The German Tradition in Philosophy

The German Tradition in Philosophy

in Philosophy

Claud Sutton

Crane, Russak & Company, Inc.
New York

First Published by Weidenfeld and Nicolson
11 St John's Hill London SW11

Published in the United States by :
Crane, Russak & Company, Inc.
52 Vanderbilt Avenue
New York, N.Y. 10017

Library of Congress Catalog Card No. 73–90539

ISBN 0–8448–0257–3

Printed in Great Britain

Contents

Preface

The present work is not intended for highly specialized philosophers, nor is it a work of original scholarship. Rather it is an individual view resulting from the work of innumerable scholars, researchers and interpreters, the result of some forty years during which I was largely engaged in the teaching of philosophy, followed by seven years in which I was otherwise occupied but had a chance of reflecting on the teaching of philosophy – how far it is worth while and why. It has also been occasioned by renewed residence in Germany, which gave me an opportunity for renewed reflection on the differences of cultural tradition within our common European culture. In this book I am frankly dogmatic on many points of interpretation which are properly disputed between scholars. I hope I have not knowingly ignored their arguments, but I decided to aim to be definite, at the risk of being wrong. I am conscious of being ignorant of some of the most recent literature.

A chief object of this work is an attempt to bridge two gaps. The first is the gap which seems to exist almost everywhere in Britain between university departments of philosophy on the one hand and departments of language and literature on the other. The work originated in the suggestion of a colleague in the German literature department that there was a need for a work on German philosophy which students of literature might be induced to read. One needs, for example, to have some knowledge of Kant in order seriously to study Schiller.

To judge from hearsay, the same gap exists between departments of philosophy and departments of English literature. Students of the latter, if they are not expected to read Hobbes, Locke, Berkeley, J. S. Mill, Bertrand Russell, miss, I believe, the enjoyment of some great writers who have shown a mastery of the English language that is inferior to none. They also miss the imaginative ideas of men who in many ways influenced the thought of an epoch – of its poets and novelists no less than of its scientists.

The other gap I have been concerned to bridge is the gap between 'subjects' of philosophy, as they have been traditionally taught. Such divisions are no doubt useful for all sorts of practical purposes – especially examinations. Traditionally philosophy has been divided into logic, theory of knowledge, philosophical psychology, scientific method, ethics, political philosophy, philosophy of history, philosophy of religion, philosophy of language – not that there is much agreement about the number and scope of these divisions! 'Metaphysics' used to be one of the recognized specialisms, but has been generally excluded since the days of Hume and Kant, who cast doubt on the quasi-mathematical proofs of the existence of God, the soul, etc. There are many who think that philosophy should now be entirely abandoned and replaced by positive sciences, especially the sciences of logical calculi and of linguistics.

I do not accept this view. It derives, I think, from the view, scotched by Hume and Kant, that philosophy is a quasi-mathematical, deductive science. The question of the value of philosophy, if any, obviously goes beyond the scope of the present work. But I see philosophy as still needed to bring together our ways of thinking about 'knowledge' – including all sorts of grades and kinds of probable belief – with our ways of thinking about social action, including communication. This conception of philosophy at any rate is a thread running through the German tradition, from Kant to Habermas, as I hope to show. To use the terms coined by Professor Strawson, I believe there is a need for philosophy as 'descriptive *and* revisionary metaphysics', having at least as much affinity to descriptive and imaginative literature as it has to natural science.

One practical matter. The German authors are the primary subjects of this work; the reader meets them, as it were, at second hand. Some readers will wish to encounter them in the original text, others in translation – for I have hopes that this book may find 'Anglophone' readers, who are not necessarily studying German. In a work of this kind many editions of each author are available, both in German and in English; it is impossible to list them all. If no translation is cited in the Bibliography, it must generally be assumed that there is none, or at least none known to me. I have not dealt in detail with purely literary sources, as this will be unnecessary for some readers and of no particular interest to others.

My chief debt is to G. W. McKay, Fellow and Tutor in German, St Peter's College, Oxford. Debts to other scholars are too numerous to mention. But among those with whom I am not personally acquainted, I should like to name Professor Walter Kaufmann of Harvard, whose works have been to me the source of many new insights.

Finally I must emphasize that this book gives one English view of the German philosophical tradition. A German certainly, an American possibly, would have stressed different aspects from those which I have stressed. One inevitably writes with one's own intellectual environment in mind.

In the intervening period between completion of this book and publication, Claud Sutton died. The publishers and Mrs Sutton are very grateful to Gilbert McKay for his assistance.

Introduction:
Are there National Traditions
in Philosophy?

'The reason that Europe can hope to work together is that our civilization is one, though our nations are several' (*The Times* leader on the European Economic Community). Whether Europe is more than a geographical expression is surely more than just a matter of the price of butter or the market for cars; we are brought up against questions of science, art, language, religion – and even philosophy, a queer subject whose right to existence is often questioned in England nowadays.

The extent of Europe in a cultural sense is also problematic. An influential writer described it as the quadrilateral formed by straight lines joining Rome, Paris, London and Berlin. This is certainly too narrow – for one thing, it excludes Edinburgh and Stockholm. Yet on the whole we may confine it to that part of Europe which was never under Turkish rule or dominated by Byzantine culture. Even so, we must certainly include nineteenth-century Russia.

Then can philosophy be European? There is obviously a good sense in which we contrast it with Indian or Chinese philosophy. But are there national styles to be found in philosophy, as there seem to be in painting and music? Is philosophy more like

I

mathematics, as some have maintained, or more like art and literature? It does seem a striking fact that in Europe there have been only three continuous, relatively independent traditions in philosophy, the British, the French, and the German. These have repeatedly influenced one another, and are as it were interlocked, and yet in many respects have gone their own way. This in my view has been true also of the American tradition which, starting with Peirce, has for the last hundred years manifested a decided character of its own, with a notable influence on the other traditions.

Since, unlike mathematics and music, the medium of philosophy is in the main ordinary language, it is bound to be much influenced by the language in which it is written; also to be influenced by, and to influence, works of poetry and of science which are written in that language. Now since about 1650, though not before, all works of philosophy have been written in national languages (though not necessarily in the mother-tongue of the author – so with Leibniz, Wittgenstein and others). This may be a clue to the way we may best speak of 'European' and 'national' in the present context. Recent philosophy has done much to illustrate the way terms necessarily take their meaning from context and contrast.

I intend to confine the conceptions of 'European' and 'British' or 'French' philosophy to the last four centuries approximately. I do not thereby for a moment subscribe to the doctrine impressed on us in my undergraduate days that medieval philosophy is of no interest or importance; nor hold that the rise of national philosophies necessarily coincides with the emergence of the political consciousness of national states. Nor that intercourse between philosophers speaking different languages suffered a sudden diminution with the close of the Middle Ages; indeed in the period we call 'the Enlightenment' it was unusually intense. Nevertheless, it is meaningful to refer to the British or French philosophy of these centuries, if we are resolute in stressing their interconnections. During these centuries Europe is indeed an *Europe des patries*, though not only, nor always, in the sense in which de Gaulle intended this phrase.

Europe was the successor of Christendom, *respublica Christiana*, just as this was successor to Greco-Roman or Mediterranean civilization. Europe in any cultural sense only came into being with the demise of Christendom, mainly with the onset of the Reformation, though of course other factors such as aspirations of princes for sovereignty contributed. And for the purposes of philosophy I propose to date Europe from the *final* demise of Christendom, for which one may take the date of the Treaty of Westphalia of 1648, which marks the end of the religious wars on the continent – in Britain the corresponding date would be 1660. Before that date we may think that the possibility of the re-establishment of some sort of unity of religion still hung in the balance – Leibniz still believed in and worked for it, until he saw that it was hopeless, and the ideal of a close union of national academies of literary men and scientists took its place in his mind. Before 1650 works of importance were still mainly written in Latin, and it still seemed to many that the new Catholicism of the Counter-Reformation might in the end prevail. Before that date the relative power of the various Protestant forms of religion – Lutheran, Reformed, Sectarian – was still very fluid. By the mid-century it was clear that the new Catholicism would survive only in half of Europe, and would not play the major part in the new forms of thought that were taking shape.

From that date Europe was a complex of sovereign states corresponding to a considerable extent with unities of language and culture. From the political point of view this new fact received its recognition in the work of Grotius (de Groot, 1583–1645), who attempted to bring some order into this new world by deriving from the old Roman ideas of *jus gentium* the quite new idea of what Bentham was later to term 'international law'.

Some might date the new self-consciousness of Europe from the Renaissance. But the Renaissance, though giving rise to such conscious Europeans as Erasmus, Leonardo, More and Bacon, remained abortive, in spite of the influence which the humanism of these men and the discoveries of others such as Kepler and Galileo exerted upon the subsequent age. Important too was the revival of a familiarity with classical imagery and of Greek scientific

3

ideals. But much of this was lost in endless theological controversies and in the religious wars which often established bigoted governments. And as has often been pointed out, the ideals of the new European science were quite different from the Greek, and called for much philosophical re-thinking. The gap of understanding which we feel in studying medieval thought, we do not feel in studying the European thought which begins in the mid-seventeenth century with Descartes and Hobbes. These may be called the fathers of the Enlightenment, that great period of scientific discovery and philosophical renewal, in which the thinkers of the next hundred years felt that they were privileged to be living.

René Descartes (1596–1650) and *Thomas Hobbes* (1588–1679) were personally acquainted, through the latter's exile in Paris. Their lives and teaching lie outside the scheme of this book, but for an understanding of the subsequent development of thought throughout Europe it is necessary to realize the extent to which they broke with previously accepted ideas and set the tone of subsequent thought. They agreed first of all in doubting received opinions (with an important exception in the case of Descartes, who explicitly refused to doubt current beliefs on religious and moral questions). Second, they agreed in taking mathematical reasoning to be the only way of attaining certainty, and so the only proper model for philosophical enquiry. Descartes, the inventor of Cartesian geometry, will only take to be true what he perceives to be so 'very clearly and distinctly' – in fact, this means, what he perceives with the rigour which we demand in the conclusions of arithmetic and geometry. And Hobbes: 'Where there is place for addition and subtraction, there is also place for reason; and where these have no place, there "reason" has nothing at all to do.'[1]

For the application of this mathematical reasoning, Descartes made way for modern mathematical physics by cutting out all the hitherto recognized types of substance – 'celestial', 'animate', 'human'; and dividing all that is into two substances only, 'extension' and 'thought' – approximately equivalent to our 'matter' and 'consciousness'. All change within the former was to be the

4

subject of mathematical calculation, and of experiment so far as needed to test the validity of alternative calculations – which however ought always to start from self-evident premises.

'Consciousness' thus became for him and his English followers a separate subject of investigation; its connection with the body – at one single point in the brain, the pineal gland* – was decidedly mysterious. On its connection with our bodies, he would only say that we are convinced that God exists, is truthful, and would not deceive us in our belief that we do each really have an individual body, which we can affect by our thought and by which we are affected. (But as God has given us no such revelation regarding the animals, they were for Descartes mere matter, and could be subjected to painful experiments without limit.)

Descartes decided not to concern himself with any questions of morality or religion, but in all such matters to submit to the laws and customs of his country. He thought he had disposed of the question of God and religion, which was so important to other philosophers of the age, by the revival of what he considered to be a knock-down quasi-geometrical proof, that 'a Being than which no greater can be conceived and who also exists, is necessarily greater than one who has all other qualities but does not exist'. This proof, commonly called the 'ontological proof', he gave in various slightly different forms. It may seem at first sight to be a straight matter of arithmetic; but these conceptions of 'existence' and 'quality' are tricky, and since Kant's time this proof has not generally been considered to be valid. Indeed, during the subsequent century, Descartes was regarded as the arch-heretic by the Church.

Descartes' view of the substance he called 'extension' or 'matter-in-motion', in which the original motion imparted to it by God was conserved for ever, was certainly wrong in detail. Moreover he had a false view of the relation of mathematics to mechanics or physics. For the latter cannot start from indubitable propositions, as that two straight lines cannot enclose a space; it has to find out by experiment which qualities are susceptible of

---

* A small gland at the centre of the brain. Descartes maintained that just at this point thought could influence the 'vital spirits' or energies of the body.

mathematical treatment, and of what sort of mathematical treatment (e.g. that 'heaviness' or degrees of elasticity can be quantified, and 'hardness' cannot). But he did enable men for the first time to think of the whole material world as one, and as amenable to human mathematics. Newton's crowning work, *Philosophiae Naturalis Principia Mathematica*, would have been inconceivable apart from Descartes.

As for Descartes' other substance, 'thought' or consciousness, he thinks of it, on the whole, as consisting of logical trains of ideas – subject to a certain amount of interference by 'passions' indeed, from which however we can always free ourselves by taking thought. His psychology does not go very deep.

Thomas Hobbes of Malmesbury is a notable English philosopher who as such belongs to the English tradition. Nevertheless some allusion must be made to him for his influence on the psychology and the political and religious thought of the succeeding epoch. His physics is not original; he accepts the general proposition of Descartes that everything external to man is matter-in-motion. But he makes motion in the human body the cause of all, or almost all, that occurs in consciousness – both of what he calls the 'involuntary motions' such as sensation, imagination, passions, and of the 'voluntary motions' such as discourse. And consciousness culminates in the 'general inclination of all mankind, *a perpetual and restless desire of power after power*, ceasing only in death'.[2] The mechanics of consciousness give rise in us to a supreme desire to preserve one's life, and this is for him the only object of practical reasoning. From this supreme goal derive his, often fascinating, ideas on politics, education, religion; for he claims to show that the only way of preserving one's life in the long run is submission to the absolute rule of a sovereign who can keep order, and who is also recognized to be the only legitimate interpreter of the rules laid down by a sovereign God. The latter's laws are to be discovered in part by reasoning upon our condition, in part by reasoning from texts of the Bible – which latter reasoning however must be the sole preserve of the sovereign. (Hobbes himself in fact manipulated scriptural texts so effectively that this method of political argument went quite out of fashion in England.)

Besides Descartes and Hobbes, a third very great man and thinker calls for our attention. I venture to call him an outsider for two reasons. In the first place, as a Jew, his background and assumptions were so different from those of the other philosophers of his time; and secondly, and more importantly, because of the delayed action which caused him to have a much greater influence upon the men of a century later than upon his own generation. *Baruch Spinoza* (or Benedict, the regular translation of the Hebrew) (1632–77) came of a family of Portuguese crypto-Jews who had taken refuge from persecution in the Netherlands, where there was a large and prosperous Jewish community. He was a Hebrew scholar, author of a Hebrew grammar and continued to attend synagogue until the age of twenty-four, when he was excommunicated with the greatest solemnity and finality for his unorthodox views on the Bible. He became the admired leader of a group of sectarian Christians, who often pressed him to accept enough money to devote more time to philosophy, but he would accept little and preferred to earn his living by the craft of grinding lenses. He refused a professorship and lived a solitary and simple life, but maintained a correspondence with many of the scientists of the day, notably with Oldenburg, the first secretary of the newly-founded Royal Society of London.

Spinoza's great work, *Ethica ordine geometrico demonstrata*, written in Latin, evidently owes its form to Descartes' novel idea that if only we were good enough at quasi-mathematical analysis and subsequent deduction, a complete and certain knowledge of the nature of things could be built up from relatively few propositions, intuited by us as absolutely certain. The whole form of his *Ethics* is modelled upon the books of Euclid; it is the most completely unified system of philosophy, or total view of the world, that has ever been written. It seems self-evident to him that the only completely independent being 'which is in itself and conceived [only] through itself' is what he calls indifferently 'God-or-Nature' – we can *see* that it makes no sense to think of two such independent 'substances', for full understanding of each would require understanding of why there should be another, and of their relation.[3] And for the same sort of reason, we can see that

God-or-Nature must have an infinite number of attributes or qualities through which it can be known. We men however happen so far to know only two, that is 'extension' and 'thought' (or matter and consciousness). We obviously do not know this by Euclidean demonstration; but that is only a limitation apparently set to our thought, which is capable of progressing from the most inadequate, everyday, view of the world through two (or three) higher degrees to the most complete and scientific view of the world – of God-or-Nature – that is obtainable from our individual particular position in God-or-Nature.

For Spinoza thinks of each of us – and indeed of every thing – as a certain slice of God-or-Nature. This in his language he calls an aggregate of modes of motion, corresponding one for one with an aggregate of modes of consciousness, 'ideas'. The difference between ourselves and animals consists in the greater range and consistency of the ideas which correspond with the greater complexity of motions going on in our body, and in its environment. For our understanding goes far beyond a mere knowledge of our own body, and can gain a more and more correct view of its place in nature, the more we learn about causal laws. Also, unlike the animals, we are self-conscious (which he calls 'having an idea of an idea') and so able to learn about the causal laws governing the course of our mind. But all this understanding is only possible because we are each a fragment of God-or-Nature.

Yet we are each a fragment which has its own *conatus*, a strong urge to maintain itself as a unity, which persists until our death. In this view he is quite unlike Descartes, and resembles Hobbes. His political views also resemble those of Hobbes; politics is for him the rational organization of individuals who naturally and inevitably seek power for themselves, but must be persuaded to seek it in a manner which is truly in accord with their enlightened self-interest. It is impossible, I think, to discover in detail which of these two very different characters most influenced the other. Hobbes was before all else a lawyer-psychologist, Spinoza a physicist-mystic. But he mentions Hobbes in letters, and had Hobbes's works in his library.

How, it may be said, can mere collections of motions, and of

8

ideas, have an urge to maintain their own identity? I think the answer for Spinoza lay in the distinction he made between God-as-active and God-as-passive – which respectively he called *Natura naturans* and *Natura naturata*. From any point in the system of nature, God can be viewed as creating, within a field of what is already created, that system of physical laws which we strive to know. But in fact, according to the most adequate knowledge that we can frame, all that is is really timeless, and follows with logical necessity from the essential nature of God, who knows all intuitively. We can only get some idea of ultimate reality as God sees it in so far as we get glimpses of what he calls *scientia intuitiva*, the highest grade of knowledge and for us humans no more than an ideal, or goal of approximation. He describes this as seeing nature under the form of eternity (*sub specie aeternitatis*). This intellectual ideal is closely bound up with his moral ideal, that of achieving 'blessedness', which is the intellectual love of God. This, he explains, is a constant will to identify oneself with God-or-Nature. The degree to which any existence affirms such will is the measure of its identity.

Any system such as Spinoza's must evidently have difficulty in getting a sense to our feelings of moral responsibility and apparent freedom. Spinoza is aware of this, and gives this metaphysical treatise arranged like a geometry textbook the title – we may think it a strange one – of *Ethics*. All is in a sense determined by the nature of God; and yet he entitles the last two sections of his book, 'Human Bondage' and 'Human Freedom', 'Bondage' is our subjection to 'passive emotions' such as fear, grief and anger; this is due to ignorance of the laws of nature and especially of our bodies, and to superstitious notions such as belief in divine punishment. The way to freedom lies above all in gaining a correct understanding of the causes of our own and other people's states of mind. His description of this way out of bondage[4] has been compared to that propagated by his co-religionist, Freud.

The free man then, after ridding himself of the passive emotions, will cultivate the 'active emotions' – above all the joy that comes from vitality of the whole person, and from active cooperation with his fellow men, especially in emancipating them from the fears

9

and hates which ignorance and superstition engender. He will gradually attain to the characteristic virtues of the free man, which are strength of mind and nobility (*fortitudo* and *generositas*). His goal, like that of the old Stoics, is active identification with the plan of God, instead of being dragged along by nature; but he lays more stress than they did on the positive seeking for sources of joy or contentment (*laetitia*). He speaks with some acerbity of the harm done by those who attribute punishment and miracles to God.

His book is not easy to read. Some of the best things in it are to be found in footnotes or corollaries. He was on the whole regarded by his immediate successors as 'the horrid atheist' – destroyer of morality as of religion by his deterministic system of thought. Even Kant uses him as the example of the saintly man who will not swerve from what his conscience dictates in spite of absolute disbelief in any sort of divine providence. It must certainly be admitted that Spinoza did not understand the difference between logical or geometrical necessity, and causal necessity (of various sorts). But his mode of thought, together with his way of life which was so truly conformed to it, has had an immense fascination for many persons of an intellectual turn of mind, and is one of the great monuments of the European spirit.

In 1676 Leibniz went to Amsterdam, begged Spinoza to let him see all that he had written, and spent a whole day in conversation with him. Of this conversation between the two greatest minds of the age no report has come down to us. Upon this incident is based the quite untenable view that Leibniz just took over Spinoza's ideas and watered them down to suit the establishment of his day.

It is not for this reason that we have devoted so much space to Spinoza, but because, while not falling into any of the national traditions – not even the Jewish – he was the incorporation of many of the ideals of the Age of Enlightenment – of the conviction that devotion to the spirit of science and abolition of old superstitions and intolerance were going to usher in a new age of human happiness. It is perhaps true that eighteenth-century thinkers looked to Locke and Newton as their models rather than to Descartes and Leibniz. But it is a mistake, common in textbooks, to label the former the Rationalists and divide them sharply from the latter, the Empiricists. They all – including Hume, usually labelled the arch-empiricist – had an immense belief in the power of Reason, searching for and sifting facts by experiment, to effect practical improvement in the lives of men. Mathematical reasoning set an ideal of rigour and completeness; but reason was viewed as a force needed to dissolve and then to reconstruct – to dissolve supposed facts derived from mere tradition and authority, and then to reconstruct men's beliefs upon data obtained by systematic experiment, in alliance with new technologies. 'The two faces of Newton' (Buchdahl) are the mathematical and the experimental; *both* are expressions of reason, the latter being 'experimental reasoning upon matters of fact' (Hume).[5]

The Age of Enlightenment manifests common characteristics running through the whole of European thought. Around the time of the French Revolution it gave way to another age with a markedly different character, common in all its different national expressions. This is commonly known as the Age of Romanticism. Around the mid-nineteenth century, there was again, it seems, a marked change, initiating the age in which we are still living. There is no agreed name for this age; I propose to call it, for reasons to be developed later, the Age of Sociologism. None of these terms is entirely satisfactory; nor is the division necessarily appropriate to other manifestations of the European spirit, such as drama or music. It is merely intended to serve as a scaffolding by means of which to display the currents of European unity running through the different national cultures, so far as these find expression in philosophy. We may for the present take this to be 'general thought about man, his society, and their place in the world, thought of the kind that takes least for granted' (Gellner).[6]

It is difficult to see the salient characteristics of an age in which one is living, but it seems to me that our thought since about the beginning of the twentieth century is dominated more than formerly by the relationship of individuals to differences of culture, of inherited language, of class, occupation, sex, of human and animal societies. In spite of our present sense of crisis and disorder – not so unusual in history as we often imagine – in spite of the dominance of two non-European super-powers and the relative powerlessness of Europe, it still seems true that Europe is a source of ideas and discoveries, and that through consciousness of our great past we may be spurred to make new efforts of thought to master our present discontents. We can indeed drown in historical research, as Nietzsche emphasized, or, as Jaspers suggested 'we can make a circuit through history in order to find out what our own opportunities are.'

An interesting question, but one by no means easy to answer, is whether there is any close correlation between the successive styles we are inclined to distinguish in philosophical thought and the changes of style we note in European art, literature or music. As the above tripartite division into 'ages' suggests, it is certainly not at all obvious that 'baroque' or 'rococo' or 'neo-classical' features are to be found in philosophy. And yet philosophy is a certain kind of literature, and it seems obvious that there is normally some communication between those who choose a more abstract and those who choose a more concrete form for the expression of their thoughts about life and their attitudes to life. Indeed interest in exploring these connections is a feature of much German philosophy, and in particular of the *Kulturphilosophie* of the early twentieth century, to which we shall have to refer. In both cases, the case of the arts and the case of philosophy, we must avoid assigning rigid dates to the beginning and end of these changes, or assuming that the change was contemporary in the different countries. There are premonitions and time-lags.

But surely it is absurd to discuss European and national philosophies before we have defined what philosophy is? I think the only satisfactory way to set about this is to look at what those writers generally known as philosophers have done. A discussion of what philosophy is will have to follow, rather than precede, this historical sketch of philosophy. One finds that the meaning of this word has changed continuously in the course of the centuries. Yet it is still possible to write a book such as G. C. Anscombe's *Three Philosophers: Aristotle, Frege and Wittgenstein*, so that it seems there must be something common to these three writers over the two thousand three hundred years that separate them.

It should be stressed that the word 'philosophy' was invented by the Greeks for an activity that was quite novel in their day; it cannot be applied without reservations to Indian and Chinese thought, brilliant as much of this is. At first it meant disinterested enquiry, ignoring current traditions, into the nature of things and of man, the Ionians emphasizing the former which they called 'physics', Socrates the latter, which soon came to be called ethics, while the idea that philosophy is closely akin to mathematics derives from Plato, who made long mathematical study a precondition for the study of philosophy, which he thought would reveal the whole world to be based upon a structure of pure forms, something like the straight line and the conic section studied in geometry. Aristotle indeed allowed that philosophy might concern itself also with generalizations which are only for the most part true – in natural history, ethics and politics. But there is a powerful tradition, deriving from Plato, of which there are excellent exponents at the present time, that philosophy is essentially concerned with logic and mathematics. However, I think logic and mathematics have suffered a change of status since the days of the Greeks; they are powerful tools, but no longer regarded as the keys to unlock all the mysteries of the universe.

So at this stage only some very vague description of philosophy can be given, for example, that it is a very persistent attempt, impelled by a sense of wonder, to think of the different aspects of the world together (Whitehead, Aristotle). But we must expect that individual writers will have very different views as to the method to be followed or the results that can be achieved. In particular we should not assume that German philosophers have accepted the method which the British tradition – but not the American – has on the whole taken to be appropriate to philosophy. The aim of the British tradition, illustrated *par excellence* in the work of the great thinkers, Hume and Russell, has been to find the ultimately certain data of our knowledge in ideas or sense-data, then show how from these we build up by reasoning the world of things and persons as we ordinarily claim to know it. If, as one often reads, the work of Sartre or Marcuse is not philosophy at all, then it must be retorted that these writers were simply not trying to do the same kind of thing as Bertrand Russell or Ryle. One should approach the German philosophers to see whether the questions they raise are interesting and important, and whether their answers are relevant to the questions. In our final chapter we shall return to the question of what philosophy is, and whether it is useful to speak of a German tradition.

Our Philosophical Heritage

Renaissance : Erasmus   Leonardo   Machiavelli   Montaigne   Bacon

Pre-Enlightenment : Descartes   Hobbes   Bayle   Pascal   Fontenelle

Enlightenment :

Britain	*France*	*Germany*	*'Outsiders'*	*Scientists*
Locke	Malebranche	Leibniz	Spinoza	Newton
Shaftesbury	Voltaire	(Wolff)	Vico	Harvey
Berkeley	Diderot	Lessing		Loevenhoek
Hume	D'Alembert	Herder		
Hutcheson	Montesquieu	Kant		
Bentham	Condillac			
Paine	La Mettrie			
	D'Holbach	(Weimar	(Cusanus)	Buffon
	Helvetius	poets)	Boehme	Laplace
	Rousseau	Fichte	(Oriental	
	Condorcet		philosophy)	Dalton

Romanticism	*French Revolution and Napoleon*			
(poets)	Chateaubriand			
Burke	Maistre	Schelling		
Godwin	Saint-Simon	Hegel		
Coleridge		(poets)		
Carlyle	Fourier	Schopen-	Kierkegaard	Darwin
M. Arnold	Comte	hauer		
J. S. Mill	Cousin	Feuerbach		
Green	Bergson	Marx, Engels		
Spencer	Durkheim	Nietzsche	Brentano	
Bradley		Husserl	Meinong	Cantor
Russell		Köhler, Koffka		Frege
		Freud		Einstein
		Dilthey		Bohr

14

Sociologism	Russian Revolution and Hitler		
Linguistic phil.		Mach	Rutherford
Wittgenstein	Ricoeur	Vienna Circle	Heisenberg
Winch	Merleau-	Heidegger	Wiener
MacIntyre	Ponty	Jaspers	Shannon
	Sartre	Horkheimer	Crick-
	Lévi-Strauss	Habermas	Wilkins
		Bloc	Watson
		Marcuse	Neumann
			Morgenstern
			Chomsky

I

The Philosophy of the German Enlightenment: Leibniz and Kant

If we have been right in finding a certain unity in the successive movements and changes we see in European thought, can we descry any distinctive character of German philosophy in the course of these movements and crises? This is a question which we can only satisfactorily answer at the end of our study. It may be that German philosophy has a distinctive character only in certain periods. But it seems to be true that German philosophy, though wide open to influences from its neighbours, has manifested some features of its own that are connected with the distinctive history of the German people. Unlike these other countries, its culture strikes one as notably polycentric. We are inclined to talk of the Jena, Königsberg or South-West German 'schools', of the Vienna Circle, in a way which does not seem appropriate to England or France – at least provided we recognize the existence of Scotland! Again, we are inclined to think of German philosophy as professorial and over-systematic; there is some truth in this and it may be attributed to some extent to the numerous universities and academies set up through the cultural rivalry of the princes. The result is many centres of culture with often a rather restricted number of interested and creative persons in each.

This state of things has drawbacks and advantages, but we may think that in times when there is good communication and much movement between the different centres, as in the eighteenth century, the advantages tend to prevail. And though the spirit of the 'school' and the *esprit de système*, as D'Alembert stigmatized it, can be stultifying, yet it provides a certain counterweight against one-sidedness. German philosophy has not on the whole fallen into the extreme one-sidedness of positive-scientism on the one hand or introspective psychologism on the other. Most writers in its different epochs have tried to give fair weight to the perceptive and the active, the emotional and the intellectual, the individual and the social aspects of the human person. Also German philosophy has tended to take seriously the oddity of the human situation, which leads us sometimes to think of 'persons in the world' and sometimes of 'the person and his world'; odd too because many of the items of the 'world' – including a lot of what we call nature, the cultivated fields, the selected animals – are partly of our human making. Reflection on these matters, and on our body – the way we know the world through it and the varying extent to which we can control it – gives rise to great doubts as to the right way to speak and think of these things. It seems perhaps true that this problem – or 'mystery' (Marcel)[1] – has been the central theme of most German philosophy. That philosophy has been on the whole anthropocentric, centred around the person and his environment.

The state of devastation in which Germany found herself in the mid-seventeenth century as the result of the religious wars and the spoliation by foreign armies singled her out from her French and English neighbours. It is generally estimated that her population had been reduced by two thirds, whole regions depopulated. The new philosophy of the Enlightenment started in France and England, but the sense of a new beginning was manifest in the exuberant optimism which characterized the thought of Leibniz and Lessing, who may be regarded as leaders of the movement in Germany. Leibniz in an early work uses the French word *éclaircissement* for the goal of philosophy, and Kant in his essay, *'Was ist Aufklärung'*,[2] defines Enlightenment as 'man's release from his self-inflicted tutelage ... the motto he adopted was *sapere aude!*' In some ways one must regard Lessing as preceding Kant because his major works were published just before the *Critique of Pure Reason*; but other reasons favour the order which we shall here adopt.

Gottfried Wilhelm Leibniz (or Leibnitz, as he spelt his name when writing in French) (1646–1716) was born when Descartes was fifty, and four years after Newton. He corresponded with almost every scientist, philosopher, mathematician and theologian in Europe. A striking exception to the common view that all German philosophy is professorial, he was as much man of affairs and diplomat as mathematician and philosopher; his immense volumes of writings are almost all 'occasional' and the greater part were only published after his death – much remains unpublished. His interests were nearly universal;* as well as being the discoverer, along with Newton, of the differential calculus and the inventor of quantificational logic (and of a calculating machine), he wrote on law, medieval history, theology and Chinese culture, in which latter he was enormously interested. As librarian of the Electoral Prince of Hanover he conducted all manner of negotiations especially with the aim of achieving reunion of the Churches; and when this seemed hopeless, the pacification of Europe through corresponding national academies of learned men.

While Leibniz's system can only be understood in the context of the revolution in thought initiated by Descartes, his whole manner of thought is in revulsion against Descartes' dualism. For him the variety of things in the world manifests above all a continuity of gradation from the smallest unit up to God. In this 'fullness of being', however, three principal types of beings can be distinguished: 'bare monads', the simplest physical particles such as our protons and electrons; 'souls', the simplest units of life, such as cells; and 'spirits', those possessing the ingredient which differentiates a person from an animal. Throughout this hierarchy there are two complementary characteristics: every unit both 'takes note of' and 'reacts to' environment – has what Leibniz

---

* 'The greatest pure intellect of whom we have any record', Broad, *Ethics and the History of Philosophy* (1952), p. 74.

called 'perception' and 'appetite'. In physics this is polarity; in living things it is stimulus-and-response; in persons it is perception (sometimes unconscious), and will.* All the ordinary things which we recognize in the world are in fact compounds of these elementary substances, the monads. The reason we regard animals and persons as wholes is because of a unique non-physical relation which he calls 'dominance', by which one monad, a soul or a spirit, dominates to a varying extent the monads which we regard as composing the body.

Dominating the whole system of monads – the world – is God, who can only be conceived by us by analogy, as akin to the highest spirit-monads, although he is also to be regarded as the organizer of the whole system, since it is his decision that there should be just this number of monads rather than any other. Each monad has from its creation a character of its own, in virtue of which it will act differently from any other in any situation. But the various situations in which it will find itself is determined by God's 'choice of the best possible world' – the best, that is, of those which are logically possible given this particular set of monads.

The oddest doctrine of Leibniz, to the modern mind, is that of the 'pre-established harmony', according to which God chose at the beginning of time just that collection of monads which – each acting according to its own nature – will produce by the end of time the best possible result. Unlike the laws of logic and arithmetic deriving from God's intellect, the laws of natural science are due only to God's choice of the best possible collection of the real units that there are. And of these only the spirits are said to act freely, although the result of their actions is foreseen (and perhaps compensated for) by God. Spirits are 'inclined though not necessitated' by the perception of some possible good; thus, in Leibniz's example, God foresaw that Judas was of a nature to be inclined to betray Jesus, and this was part of his plan for the world. It may well be thought that this is an over-optimistic view of evolution and history – the assurance that there will be compensation in the future for all apparent evils of the present, which are

---

* He was the first philosopher to recognize the importance of what is unconsciously perceived (*petites perceptions*).

due to the exuberant variety of the creation. It is however one version of a belief found in many cultures and ideologies.

Leibniz was the first philosopher to point out the essential difference between laws of nature and laws of mathematics, thus going beyond Descartes and Spinoza and leading on to Hume, as the latter recognized; however much we may utilize mathematics in discovering, and again in formulating, the laws of nature, we can always imagine these to be different from what they are found to be. Laws of nature are what we have first discovered and then linked up, to form our conception of nature. And Leibniz maintains that they are but generalizations, summing up as it were the activities of the monads, the ultimate units-of-action which there are in the world. So that the laws expressing the free fall of a body, or the displacement of one body by another, express only 'well-grounded phenomena' – a term which, as we shall see, was destined to play a large part in Kant's account of the world.

Leibniz's strange scheme attempts to give an account both of the apparent unity of nature – of the subjection of human consciousness both to the laws of thought and to the laws of nature (though in different senses) – and also of man's peculiar relation to his body, with his subjective sense of freedom, and with the quite peculiar constraint exercised upon him by his perception of possible good, or value. This scheme of thought was basic for Leibniz's great inventions of the differential calculus and truth-functional logic. To the modern mind it relies rather too much on the conception of God, and claims to know too much about how He holds the totality of things together. Nor does Leibniz's account of the unity of the person in his environment seem entirely satisfactory. The very stimulating philosophy of A.N.Whitehead in *Process and Reality* is a modernized version of Leibniz.

Leibniz was the first person since the ancients to explore the oddities of space and time. Space-relations ('two miles', 'up', 'left') are meaningless except in the context of things-in-space, yet they are *not* qualities of the things; and the same is true of temporal relations. Leibniz observed that if God had made the world twice as big, or a fortnight earlier than he did, no one could know it, and it would make no difference to any perception or action whatever. 'Empty space' and 'empty time' are not nothing, but they are very peculiar things or concepts; Leibniz called space and time 'phenomena of God'. This was to start Kant on the way to some of the central concepts of his philosophy.

Immanuel Kant (1724–1804) was the very type of the professorial philosopher, spending all his life as a teacher at the university of his native Königsberg. In consequence he employs many technical terms arising out of the academic controversies of the time, and this results in many difficulties of interpretation for the reader (see glossary appended to this chapter). Yet his thought is still alive today, so that it seems worth while to make a ruthless attempt to cut through some of these difficulties. His main motive is to explain the prodigious yet somehow orderly variety of things in the world, and also the peculiar place in it of persons who are somehow responsible for some of their actions. The main difference of interpretation is between those who see a close connection between the two sides of his work (as I do) and those who do not.

Kant is the originator of one of the main themes of present-day philosophy, the question of how much our common view of the world is due to conventions of thought and language. He starts by postulating, as Leibniz did, two levels of reality. These he calls 'appearances' or 'phenomena', contrasted with 'things-themselves' or 'noumena' (lit. 'thinkables'). (These pairs of terms are not exactly equivalent – 'things-themselves' are only one sort of 'thinkables' – but the basic contrast he wants to stress is much the same.) We can, indeed must, *think* that there are some things which are perceived only partially; again of unperceived trends and tendencies; of what is imagined; of characters not perceived at all, but expressed in action. His central doctrine is that our common-sense view of an orderly world is due to the human person, who is active in perception, synthetizing or holding together his fragmentary and fleeting bits of experience, according to some detectable rules which Kant calls 'categories'; and always guided by the postulate that there is only one standard uniform space and time accessible to all, within which our experiences must be correctly located if they are to count as real.

But the person is active too in another way altogether, when he tries to do what he conceives to be right. The clearest case of this is where he feels obliged by an unconditional moral principle like 'I couldn't possibly desert her now.' Exactly how these two activities, learning and practice, and certain others we shall refer to, are connected is a question at the very core of Kant's philosophy. As well as the image of ourselves which we perceive in a mirror and which we get to know further through science, we have in moral action, but also in scientific research and cultural creation, some experience of ourselves as a 'noumenal' – we are originators, not just passive recipients.

Physical objects like stones, on the other hand, are just 'standardized phenomena'. Now 'standardized' means that we have to think of them as (1) *unaffected by their mere position* in space and time; (2) *measurable* against one another; (3) in some sense *substantial* or identifiable when we meet them again; (4) not changing without some cause – these are the 'categorical' aspects which an experience must have to count as real, not merely a subjective or illusory apparition. Many subsequent philosophers have utilized this conception of categories though not exactly as Kant did.*

In physical science, which is a refinement of ordinary experience, he maintains that there are similar and connected factors, which he calls axioms or principles. These again are required because of the peculiar features of space and time, and consist in axioms about the possibility of quantitative and qualitative measurement; which exclude, e.g. the possibility of our measuring rods shrinking undetectably as we move them about; and in the three principles: of conservation, universal-causality and reciprocal-action-and-reaction. Most people agree about the significance of these principles, though their interpretations vary; in particular, it may be debated whether the statistical laws employed in nuclear physics and for many other scientific purposes are a kind of causal law or not.

To anyone familiar with the *Critique of Pure Reason*, it must be evident that in giving this account of Kant's doctrine of the conventional or human element in all our experience, and of his 'two level' view of the world as consisting of phenomena and

---

* Mundle thinks that the indispensable categories are: thing, event, process, time, space, body, mind, person (*A Critique of Linguistic Philosophy*).

things-themselves, I have skated over innumerable difficulties and disputes. The *Critique*, especially its first half which gives Kant's doctrine of the nature of experience and of science, really is a difficult book to read, even in conjunction with one of the numerous commentaries which exist.* For those who wish to explore further Kant's theory of convention in our experience, one may recommend the *Prolegomena to any Future Metaphysic*, which he wrote as his own popularizing elucidation of the *Critique*. (Except that one particular section (Part II, section 18) is erroneous, out of line with the major work, and should be disregarded.) In the *Critique of Pure Reason*, a non-specialist reader should ignore (*a*) all that Kant writes about logic – the sections called the 'Transcendental Clue', the 'Metaphysical Deduction of the Categories', 'The Derivation of Dialectic from the Three Sorts of Syllogism', all of which was to impress the learned public of his time, but is erroneous, and unimportant for his general argument; (*b*) all that he writes about the psychology of sensations and understanding, e.g. about sensibility handing over to understanding and this to reason, especially in the first edition of the 'Deduction of the Categories', which is based upon a superseded faculty-psychology and does not really help his main argument at all.

The reader's lifeline in reading the most difficult central section of the 'Analytic' – the first half of the *Critique of Pure Reason* – is that Kant's novel principle is that each person experiences himself as a continuing consciousness or subject of experience; now, if you think about it, this presupposes some features in the world we experience – first and foremost, that it consists of identifiable things which we are able to recognize again as the same things. Such recognizing is a case of what he calls 'combining' or 'synthetizing', and time and space being as they are, it involves an *activity* of holding past and present together. (What he says in detail about the way our mind holds together, inner sense and outer sense, etc., can well be ignored.)

Such is the general argument of the section called 'Transcendental Deduction of the Categories'. But the position of this sec-

---

* There are many recent commentaries on the first half of Kant's work, but very few which attempt to bring the whole together.

tion is most unfortunate. As to what these permanent features of the experienced world must be, and their relation to space and time, that we can discover far more satisfactorily from the subsequent section, called 'Analytic of Principles'. As the result of an undoubtedly erroneous idea about logic, he conceived that he had to deduce the principles (of measurability, identifiability, explicability in terms of laws, and possibility) – first from what he called 'schematized categories'; then these from 'schemata'; then these from 'unschematized' categories; then these from tables of judgements as found in the currently approved logic books! In all this there is much of interest to scholars, but in the account of what he called his Copernican argument, from the nature of the person to the nature of the world as experienced it does not help, and can be ignored by the non-specialist.

What Kant has to say about mathematics and its applicability is also of much interest, but its discussion would take us beyond the bounds of the present work. He contends:

(1) that pure geometry and pure arithmetic, though arising out of facts of our sense-experience, can give rise to 'constructions' which provide us with absolutely universal and necessary propositions – when we draw figures or calculate;

(2) that we then find that they are applicable to experience, enabling us to formulate laws of nature. (Kant was quite aware that different geometries are thinkable.) This applicability shows that they are a kind of grid through which all human beings inevitably see things; that *uniform* space and time are not themselves qualities of the ultimate things-themselves. It is important to take what he says at the beginning in the 'Aesthetic' in connection with what he later says in the 'Analytic' of principles, and the antinomies.

Kant maintains, then, that both in science and in ordinary experience we do not know the identity of the real sources of action as they are in themselves, but only as they must appear to any human being. Noumena are problematic; this is because we perceive them within the matrix or grid of uniform space and time. Yet that gives rise to inevitable logical contradictions (the antinomies) when we think, as we are bound to do, about 'the first event' 'the smallest item in the world', 'universal causal laws' and 'causal activity'. These contradictions worry us most in our own case – how to reconcile the causal laws of physics and those of juristic thought – but also in thinking about other living creatures which manifestly *behave* as unities; and even in thinking about the elementary particles of physics. Persons act into space and time; they do not occupy a determinate piece of space and time; and the same seems to be true of the elementary particles.

Nor can we be content just to establish a number of particular laws of nature and leave it at that. Kant maintains that in learning about the world we are driven on by three assumptions that we take for granted (the 'ideas of reason'): that there is *to be discovered* a systematic unity of the human person, a systematic unity of physical nature and a systematic unity of all the beings there are, which latter he terms 'God'. This is not knowledge but practical belief, implied by our researches and our urge to push them further.

It is widely agreed since Kant that there are indeed some conventional elements in our everyday views about the world; many moderns regard this as due to our having certain words like 'thing', 'cause', 'persons', available to us in the language we take over as children. But it may well be that, with all the variety of languages that we find in the world, there is some 'deep structure' (as Chomsky calls it), e.g. that in any language whatever there must be nouns and verbs; which structure makes human language possible and corresponds to Kant's categories. It was Kant's younger contemporary Herder who was the first to think much about such questions (see chapter 2).

Equally fundamental for Kant is that we do know, or at any rate experience, ourselves sometimes as free agents, on a different plane from the objects of ordinary experience and of science, different again from trains of sensations or perceptions, the way David Hume pictured us. We act into the world, manifesting a different kind of causality from that we attribute to physical phenomena. Kant thinks that the idea of a cause or explanation of a whole series of events is quite intelligible to us: 'If I for instance arise from my chair in complete freedom, a new series of events with natural consequences *ad infinitum* has an absolute beginning in this event.'* He thinks that in many situations we know that talk about the immediate physical antecedents is quite irrelevant as an explanation of a human action:

> Ask a man whether it would be possible for him to overcome his love of life, however great it may be, if his sovereign threatened him with sudden death unless he made a false deposition against an honourable man whom the ruler wished to destroy on some plausible pretext. Whether he would do so or not, perhaps he will not venture to say; but that it would be *possible* for him he would certainly admit without hesitation. He judges therefore that he can do something because he knows that he ought to, and recognizes that he is free, a fact which without the moral law would have remained unknown to him.[3]

There are some who hold – misinterpreting this last sentence – that Kant sets an impassable gulf between knowing what is true on the one hand and acting morally on the other hand. But I think this interpretation is false, for it ignores all that he writes about scientific research, about culture, about art, about the wider aspects of morality and about its relation to religion. 'Man knows himself in acts and inner determinations, which he cannot regard as impressions of the senses.'[4] Nor, one may add, as a sum of physiochemical pressures.

It is often alleged that Kant held that we are only free when acting in obedience to moral rule; that in all other cases, either when acting badly or constructing something, our apparent act is not free, but just the result of physical laws. This view is plainly nonsensical, although in his early but influential work, *The Moral Law* (*Grundlegung*), he does appear to take it. It would mean that we could never really *do* anything wrong; that would be just something that happens to us. But Kant does think that we all sometimes have clear unconditional obligations; the fact that man alone of creatures is capable of suffering and even of dying for an unconditional principle is the most persuasive argument for man's freedom. Kant

* I agree with J. R. Lucas that recent developments in thought – Gödel's theorem and quantum mechanics – have rendered a rigorously deterministic view of the world not simply unprovable, but even logically untenable. See MacIntyre, *Marcuse* (1970), especially the last chapter and the one on self-inclusive classes.

does not think it is the only argument, or that freedom is a mere practical postulate, on a par with God and immortality (which he sometimes mentions in the same context); 'freedom proves its objective reality in Nature by means of the effects it produces there.'[5]

Within the sphere of human willed action, Kant certainly thought it important to distinguish what he called pure or autonomous moral action – where we seem subject to a law requiring us to act in a certain way 'though the heavens fall', without calculation of what is most likely to result or consideration of our inclinations – from a wider sphere, that of art, culture and community life, in which, as he says, reason is operative though not legislative[6] – a sphere of maxims and counsels, not laws. This is developed in his later books, *Critique of Judgement* and *Religion within the Bounds of Reason Alone*. Both art and technique, he says, involve an element of practical reason; 'if we call the regular cells of bees a work of art, this is only by analogy; as soon as we feel that no rational consideration went to their construction, we say it is a product of Nature or instinct.' The product of art is a symbol of moral goodness because it makes an unconditional claim that its existence is worth while, and appeals to us apart from all possible utility.

Besides the field of art, he refers to culture as the other great field in which reason is operative – surprisingly, he does not include art in culture. This he divides into the 'culture of skill . . . which however is not sufficient for the determination and choice of purposes'; and the 'culture of training, or discipline . . . which consists in freeing the will from the despotism of desires'. These two are prerequisites of morality, 'for they alone make possible a civil community in which lawful authority is opposed to the abuse of conflicting freedoms'. Yet culture without individual sense of moral responsibility can only produce the splendid misery of senseless luxury. To win our unconditional approval, culture must include a moral ideal.

Kant is often criticized for the extreme rigorism of his views on morality. He tells us in his early work that moral laws apply both in this world and out of it; but a morality which has no material of human needs and desires to bite on is surely irrelevant to our situation. He wants to say, I think, that (as with particular scientific laws by contrast with the 'categories') in morality there is a difference between maxims based on experience, which will usually tend to produce a good life in a particular community or in an individual at a particular stage of development, and principles, recognition of which is basic to any sort of moral community. These principles are in the first place truthfulness and fidelity – for I cannot even 'think a community' in which people tell lies and break promises absolutely at random – and in the second place self-help and willingness to help others, without which, he says, I could not *will* that any community should exist.[7] Would I be willing that the principle on which I propose to act should be adopted universally? Such principles are in some sense axiomatic, like the categories; for they make possible reflection upon social life and evaluation of human action from a moral point of view. (One may be uncertain into which class justice or equity falls; but I think this is because the concept has a minimal as well as a maximal or ideal sense. We cannot begin to judge any action without assuming that the relevant needs of all concerned must be taken into account. But when Kant asserts that man's highest good is to seek to reconcile justice and happiness, he is using the concept 'justice' in a wider sense – and intends that we should aim at something more than a minimal degree of fairness. The man who steadfastly pursues this aim will not necessarily be happy, but he will, Kant says, be content.)

In *Religion within the Bounds of Reason Alone* Kant develops his mature view about a moral disposition (*Gesinnung*), and the ways and degrees of degeneration and regeneration of our power of acting morally, in face of our natural desires and of our proper demand for happiness. He rejects the notion of any man being born naturally evil; life can be a vicious spiral of increasing degeneration, but a man can never completely shake off the feeling of a duty to rehabilitate himself, and what man can feel as an imperative must be possible in some sense. One may say that Kant distinguishes between man's duty and freedom to do what is obligatory here and now; and, contrasting with this, his duty and freedom to 'progress towards a good disposition', and to choose such goals as tend towards the establishment of an ethical community ('a kingdom of persons considered as ends in themselves').[8]

This brings us to the final stage of Kant's thought, about what he calls 'the possible common ground of phenomena and noumena, which may not be so heterogeneous after all' – what he calls the 'postulates of practical reason' – immortality and God. About the former he does not say much; it is an argument from man's disposition, a steady desire to progress in morality (or knowledge) as something that is not strictly in physical time – 'its existence is not susceptible of division into periods of time but must be viewed as a temporal unity, a whole.' So that no fully-human person can say: 'Well, if I am just going to die, what does my last act matter?' or (like Ibsen's bishop in *The Pretenders*): 'I can do all the evil I want, provided I manage to repent at the last moment.' The good man should be at any rate willing to have another life, not fear it, and the particular moment of his death will be unimportant for him. I think this is really just an argument from the good man's belief in the worthwhileness of life, which cannot be estimated by regarding it as algebraic sum of moments of happiness and moments of unhappiness.* Kant has singularly little to say about the possibility of continued life with or without a body, holding that we are totally ignorant about the nature of the communion between thought and will on the one hand and body on the other.[9] All we know is that the former are operative *into* space and time, and not to be satisfactorily described in terms of spatio-temporal measurements and of the physical laws based on such measurements.

He has a good deal more to say about God as a 'practical postulate'. He was clearly not content to have demolished (as most people think he has done) the traditional proofs of the existence of God. He argues (in the 'Fourth Antinomy') that a cause of a different kind for the endless causal series of contingent events in space and time is both 'a demand of reason' and inconceivable. Practical reason demands further research *ad indefinitum* to link

* 'Is the will for transcendence of death the very kernel of religion?' (George Steiner in BBC lecture).

up phenomena, on the assumption that nature is fundamentally one and rational. Practical reason needs not only 'limiting concepts' (*Ideen*) such as 'the infinite' and 'the infinitesimal', but ideals also (*Ideale*), 'standards . . . providing it with a concept of that which is entirely complete in its kind'. Such an ideal of reason is God. His existence can be proved neither from conceptual analysis (the ontological and cosmological proofs) nor by induction from the orderliness of nature (the teleological proof) – the latter is of philosophical significance, but it does not prove the existence of anything like the traditional all-powerful and all-good God. Kant, though child of the Age of Enlightenment, lived in a time of reaction against Leibniz's optimism, and makes plenty of references to the seeming lack of a good order in the world, e.g. he writes somewhere that the production of human souls seems to be largely due to chance and vice.[10]

Kant postulates God as necessary to harmonize happiness and morality; is he therefore just going back on his fundamental doctrine that morality is unconditional obedience to a principle, whether it pays or not, on earth or in heaven? His true doctrine is to be found, I believe, in the *Critique of Judgement* (especially, section §87). If one considers not just the individual's moral acts, but his cooperation with other persons (and Kant would say also with the animals and the plants) as being effective, not illusory, then one must suppose it possible to realize some common good of them all, which he calls 'happiness in accord with morality'. Morality has insufficient content unless we assume that human happiness or welfare is good in itself; but analysis of the utilitarian concept of maximum happiness has conclusively shown that this makes no sense unless one makes some assumptions about fair distribution and non-deception – but these are assumptions derived from morality.*

Now Kant asserts that the man who is completely sceptical about the course of the world, who believes it (like Camus) to be absurd, 'owing to the many irregularities of nature', will feel still no less obliged to fulfil individual duties to his neighbours. 'If persuaded of the proposition "there is no God" he would

---

* Cf. Arrow, *Social Choice and Individual Values* (1963, 2nd ed.).

nevertheless be contemptible in his own eyes if on that account he looked on the laws of duty as empty, invalid, inobligatory.' 'No!' says Kant, 'in such a case he will only give up aiming at that final purpose in the world which is to be brought about by pursuing the happiness of rational beings in harmony with the pursuit of moral laws'[11] – as he calls it elsewhere, 'working for the possibility of an ethical community'. What this amounts to, I think, is that the man who, beyond fulfilling his clear duties, works in the hope of the uncertain and long-term good of his fellow men, must believe both that sub-human nature is not intractable nor ultimately hostile to man, and that in the long run morality and happiness are not incompatible. Kant holds this to be equivalent to belief in God, the 'ultimate X' that links natural law and moral law.*

Is this just a gross abuse of the term 'God'?† I venture to think that men do not pursue long-term cooperative purposes involving great discipline and self-sacrifice, except on some metaphysical or religious assumptions, often perhaps hardly formulated. There is certainly some such metaphysical assumption in Marxism. It is an assumption about the significance of man and his activity, as 'eye and speech of an otherwise dark and dumb world' (Jaspers). Of course, Kant has a good deal more to say about the meaning of the concept 'God' in the context of historical religion – which he thinks may equally lead either to the purification or to the degradation of morality ('fanatical religion'). But he is sure that morality cannot be based upon revelations, and that any belief in God is a metaphysical assumption that depends on taking man's nature as a moral being seriously. He was prepared to allow that positive religion plays a part in persuading us that this 'ultimate X' God is a 'power making for righteousness'.

Kant is difficult to read; is he worth it? He is full of good observations, especially in his *Critiques* of Judgement and of Practical Reason. He is, I believe, 'relevant for us' because most of the time he is wrestling with Hume's empiricism – Hume's narrow view of experience as a collection of sense-impressions.

* Cf. Einstein, '*Raffiniert ist der Herrgott, aber böse ist er nicht*' ('Very subtle is the Lord God, but malicious he is not'), inscription at Harvard University.

† Cf. 'Religion is the expression of human aspiration' (W. Kaufmann).

Experience contains an element of human convention, is the only final test of scientific truth, is a boundary to us, but never 'entirely enough for reason'. At the start he is concerned to establish the proposition that we only 'know' in the strict sense of the word appearances or phenomena in space and time; not that which we 'think of' as appearing (*noumenon*). But it gradually emerges from his work that we distinguish importantly different kinds of appearances, such as rocks, numbers, masses, organisms, pictures, consciousness; and that we 'think of' importantly different kinds of *noumena* or thinkables: the things-themselves which he says affect us in perception; living beings; persons; communities of persons; God. The only common characteristic of all these thinkables is that they are not literally 'in' space and time. But it turns out that, even if we cannot know, there is quite a lot we can reasonably believe about these various thinkables – they are not just fictions about which we haven't a shadow of evidence one way or another. In most contexts, a 'real thing' means the sum of its apparent changes within a certain slice of space and time. But this level of reality points beyond itself.

In other contexts, we have to recognize free persons and the products of their community, such as language and art, as realities of another sort, without which the former level, of 'appearances', is not fully intelligible.

On a third level we must think the different conjectural entities which manifest themselves in space and time – animals and plants, viruses, the various elementary particles, mesons, pions, etc. Just what we should recognize as the ultimate units, and their relation to one another, is very dubious, but we can't avoid thinking of them; it certainly seems as if nature cannot be reduced to a geometry, describing only what patterns of change are found in different areas of space and time. Philosophers from Descartes onwards have tried out this mode of thought; it does not work.

Kant is often thought of as attaching too much importance to morality; and indeed when one thinks of all we now know about moral differences in different cultures, he should have developed more than he did the connection between what is seen as fitting and desirable in given circumstances, and what is unconditionally obligatory. Fortunately, life does not consist only of duties; but a sense of duty does seem to be the basis for any fully personal life – and most certainly for any kind of science, which depends on unconditional respect for truthful communication. This, as Kant saw, involves one in a metaphysical view about the relation between man and nature. Whether to call his philosophy the critical destruction of metaphysics, or a new 'Metaphysics of Experience' was a matter on which he could not make up his mind.

Thus, although he spent much of his time criticizing Leibniz, I think Kant's view of the world is still akin to and developed out of that of Leibniz; he believes that there are many centres of energy each manifesting some measure of free causation, and that among the various sorts of these, the human person is of cardinal significance. He wrote at the end of his life: 'The *Critique of Pure Reason* is after all the real apologia for Leibniz, even against his followers who . . . do him no honour.'[13]

It is not too much to say that subsequent German philosophy hinges upon the work of Kant, and that understanding of him is vital for any understanding of European philosophy. He was the first to show clearly the essential ambiguity of man's status in the world.* But his account of this status leaves many tantalizing gaps to be filled. What is the relation between the synthetizing activity of mind in cognition and its manifestation in practical action? Is the individual human mind (as I believe Kant thought) operative in both fields? Or is it some super-individual mind, as his term 'transcendental logic' suggested, and as his successors were to assert? If the individual human mind is operative in cognition, how is it that we achieve the notion of one world common to all percipients, and communicate with one another about this world? Is there such a thing as practical reason, and what is the relation between the sphere in which it is legislative (morals) and the sphere in which it is operative (art, social institutions). These were the questions which were to be taken up by his philosophical successors, Fichte, Schelling, Hegel and Schopenhauer, often called the 'German Idealists'.

* Developed especially by Jaspers.

But before coming to these we must take note of another tradition, outside the faculties of philosophy, which to a certain extent offered answers to these questions, culminating in the classical literature of the court of Weimar and its university of Jena.

Here, as a bridge, we may mention Kant's little work of 1784, *Ideas on General History, as leading to World-Citizenship*,[14] as illustrating his mature views upon the cooperation of natural law and free-will in history, and his relation to Herder's and Hegel's philosophy of history. He starts by saying that the marriage statistics show how little the act of marriage, which is supposed to be an outcome of human reason, is in fact governed by reason; it is far more a product of natural conditions, of plenty and dearth, and so on. 'For in man Reason is only effective in the species as a whole', not in an individual life. For all the possible powers of human nature to be brought to fruition, 'Nature requires that there should be antagonisms in society. Thanks be to Nature for man's insatiable desire to possess and to rule!' 'Man needs a master who will be just towards himself . . . and a complete solution of this is impossible.' But a good civil constitution, and the building up of respect for inter-state law can provide conditions in which both natural struggle and the prevalence of morality which is essential for culture are alike possible.

'Philosophy can have its utopias', and an arcadian life of perpetual peace and harmony should not be one of them. Strife within limits is good. 'The idea of a world-history which has a sort of *a priori* clue is a legitimate speculation of reason.'

Kant is an originator. His doctrine of the effects of our assumption of uniform space and time upon our interpretation of the world; of the place of categories in interpreting experience; of the test of 'universalizability' in moral action – these are the starting point of many modern discussions of the nature of science and the nature of morality. So he is worth making some effort to read.

Glossary

Technical terms for those intending to read the *Critique of Pure Reason*, the *Critique of Practical Reason*, the *Critique of Judgement*, the *Prolegomena*, or the *Foundation of the Metaphysic of Morals* in German, *Grundlegung der Metaphysik der Sitten* – variously translated into English).

Aesthetic, concerned with the data of the bodily senses (not with art)

Amphiboly, ambiguity of meaning

Analytic, concerned with judgements or propositions; analytic judgements are self-evident apart from all experience

Antinomy, contradiction resulting from two different lines of reasoning

Apperception, consciousness (in its simplest form)

A priori, not derived from experience

Autonomous act, completely free act of will

Canon, standard of correct reasoning

Categorical duty, a duty regardless of considerations of happiness

Category, a conception necessary for the understanding of *any* judgement about experience

Dialectic, reasoning which leads to conclusions that contradict other equally-rational conclusions

Heteronomous, act or decision determined by circumstances or inclination

Hypothetical duty, a duty, if one presumes a desire for happiness of the individual

Intuition, a source of knowledge or an element in knowledge not requiring use of understanding or reason found in all perception and in mathematics

Modality, possibility, probability, necessity

Organon, model or device for correct reasoning

Paralogism, mistake in a train of reasoning

Pure, same sense as *a priori*

Schema, a simplified diagram or model

Synthetic, characterizing judgements or propositions involving the relating-together of different experiences

Teleology, apparent design or purpose manifest in a set of facts

Transcendent, beyond the bounds of experience, unknowable

Transcendental, relating to the necessary features of all experience

Understanding, the power of applying concepts or rules correctly

2

The German Enlightenment: Lessing, Herder and Weimar

Gotthold Ephraim Lessing (1729–81) is an important figure if we are to form a rounded picture of the philosophy of the German Enlightenment. A Saxon, he studied theology at the University of Leipzig, but soon abandoned this for play-writing, which was his first interest. He criticized the artificiality of the French theatre, advocated the study of Shakespeare and wrote the well-known plays, *Minna von Barnhelm*, *Emilia Galotti*, and finally *Nathan der Weise*, which last reflects much of his philosophy of life – including the famous parable of the three rings – and his close friendship with the Jewish writer, Moses Mendelssohn.

For us, Lessing represents another important side of the German Enlightenment, for his interest was less in natural science than in history and theology, in which he strove 'to free man from his self-inflicted tutelage'. Influenced by the Frenchman Pierre Bayle, who had covertly and slyly criticized Christianity in his *Dictionnaire* (1686), and by the Englishman Locke's *Reasonableness of Christianity* (1695), he published and supported the work of Reimarus, the first writer to apply rational principles of historical criticism to Christianity. This led Lessing to develop a philosophy of history in his *Education of the Human Race* (*Die Erziehung des*

37

Menschengeschlechts) (1780). Just as there is a necessary order in which instruction can be imparted to the child, he claimed, so there is a necessary order in the revelation of God to the human race. The Old Testament is like the first of the child's primers; the New Testament like the primer of a higher stage; each is loaded with doctrines valuable for their time, but later to prove harmful; the third age, of truthful religion, is yet to come. Above all, like Spinoza, he rejects the idea of punishment by God. This concept should be replaced by a belief in reincarnation, in which in the course of many lives the individual would be gradually educated regarding the effects of his good or evil deeds.

Lessing's utopia however is not a world-state like Kant's, nor a universal religion; in his *Dialogues* and in the ring parable of *Nathan der Weise* he shows that he regards clashes and rivalries as creative and necessary. Again, in his clear separation of historical fact from philosophical truth he anticipates later thinkers. 'Christianity', he writes, 'is a religion whose historical truth looks dubious', but it can convey important inner truths; for 'there can be a rational content in mysteries'. Thus, though primarily in relation to religion, he develops a view that there is something intelligible to be discovered in the succession of different cultures in history. (His *Laokoon* helped to develop that theory of the primacy of classical art which played so large a part in later Weimar.)

J. G. Herder (1744–1803) took philosophical thought on these topics a good deal further. His treatise of 1772, '*Ueber den Ursprung der Sprache*' ('On the Origin of Language'), is a landmark. Language, he maintains, is not to be attributed to divine creation, but develops gradually as man begins to use his native powers of thought. There are primitive, poetical and finally philosophical types of language. He stresses that 'language is due to the totality of all human powers, cognitive and volitional'.[1] Language then is seen as filling the gap Kant had left between cognition and will. It is also the primary explanation of the power to communicate with other human beings, and to form a society in collaboration with them, a matter on which Kant had not much to say. All thinking for Herder is 'inward speaking', and the very first human thought is aimed to communicate with another. (The wild children brought up by animals are for ever incapable of human language.) There is indeed a diversity of human languages, but he claims that they all derive from a common source; so that, difficult as it may often be, we do take it for granted that communication through language with another human being is always possible.[2]

His researches into the nature of language naturally led him into the philosophy of history, in which he had been preceded to some extent by the Neapolitan Vico and by Montesquieu (*Esprit des Lois*, 1748). This he expounded in *Ideen zu einer Philosophie der Geschichte* (1884-91). The differences of language make it clear to him that 'every age and culture has its own value, which the historian must view without partiality and judge without passion.' As well as its own language, each people also has its own mythologies; 'for the shepherd sees Nature with different eyes from the fisherman or the hunter.' This naturally brings with it clashes of interest: 'Man starts to be unsociable when his own natural interests clash with those of other men'; this can only be countered by the development of good traditions, 'for the happiness of man everywhere is climatic and organic, and the child of tradition and custom', conceptions very different from those of Kant. However, he agrees with Kant that 'the striving for happiness concerns the individual alone, not the species nor the state.'

Herder is resolutely against what he regards as pantheism ('the Averrhoan system') – against the 'absolute' which plays so large a part in Fichte, Schelling and Hegel; he emphasizes that the gaps in Kant's account of man can quite well be explained in terms of culture and language – 'culture' being understood in what is now often called the anthropological sense of the term as the totality of valued habits, customs, institutions and works of a society. He regards this growth more as a matter of gradual continuous change than of sudden revolutions; 'only a few men add links to the chain of tradition' (an early hint of the Romantic theory of the genius).

Unlike Kant, he sets no great gulf between morality and culture; culture has for him a moral aspect. 'Man is constituted for humaneness (*Humanität*) and for religion.' Religion however for Herder was what we should probably label as evolutionary humanism;

he interprets salvation in a purely ethical sense, and revelation as the contribution to the cultural tradition which is made by great men, including poets and philosophers. Christianity, he says, was 'thrown into the seething mixture of the European tradition for better or for worse'. Jesus was a man influencing the current ideas of his time with the aim of 'directing the mind towards nobler thoughts'. It is surprising, given the common attitude of other governments, that Duke Karl August and Goethe managed to keep him in office as General Superintendent (supreme authority in Lutheran Church affairs) until his death; equally surprising that Herder consented to the expulsion of Fichte from his post as professor, on the charge of atheism.

This ethical ideal of *Humanität* (for which there is no easy translation), arising out of a providential tradition ennobled by the work of certain great individuals, was a major element in the Weimar classicism of Goethe and Schiller. For them it signified above all the harmonious development of all the faculties of man, and was to be achieved primarily by efforts of self-education (*Bildung*) of each individual. And religion usually means for them an idealized religion such as that of Greece, illustrated for example in Goethe's *Iphigenie* and Schiller's *Die Götter Griechenlands* – religion as source of an ideal culture. *Humanität* may be said to be the main inspiration of Schiller's dramas, and of the literary form of Goethe's *Bildungsroman*. Schiller, the great idealist, is the exponent of *Humanität* in his anti-Kantian and philosophically important essay, 'Ueber Anmut und Würde' ('On Grace and Dignity'), in which he criticizes Kant's moral rigorism, and stresses the expressive significance of many actions which at first sight have nothing to do with morality.[3]* The truly moral man according to Schiller is not one who is always obedient to laws, but one who shows graciousness in action, and dignity in suffering.

Goethe's inspiration may rightly be called a humanism, but it is a good deal more complex and profound than that of Schiller. He was, or aimed to be, a scientist and administrator as well as a poet, and he gave more recognition to the wilder aspects of human nature, joys and sorrows, that are not so readily harmonized.

* Cf. Sartre's 'existential preferences', *L'Etre et le Néant*, p. 690.

Schiller could hardly have written the 'Harper's Song'.* Faust is scarcely a harmonious character, and his final epitome of wisdom† signifies endless struggle in which alone is salvation.§ Goethe's own view of philosophy is most succinctly given at the end of *Poetry and Truth*:

> The child, the boy, the youth sought by various ways to approach the supernatural; first looking with strong inclination to a religion of nature; then clinging with love to a positive one; and finally concentrating himself in the trial of his own powers and joyfully giving himself up to a general faith ... He thought he could detect in Nature – both animate and inanimate, with soul and without soul – something which manifested itself only in contradictions, and which therefore could not be comprehended under any one idea, still less under one word. It was not godlike, for It seemed without

Wer nie sein Brot mit Tränen ass
Wer nie die kümmervollen Nächte
Auf seinem Bette weinend sass
Der kennt euch nicht, ihr himmlischen Mächte!

Ihr führt ins Leben uns hinein.
Ihr lasst den Armen schuldig werden.
Dann überlasst ihr ihn der Pein.
Denn alle Schuld rächt sich auf Erden.

(Who never ate with tears his bread,
Who never sat the care-full hours
Of night crying upon his bed:
He has not known you, Heavenly Powers!

You gave us life, and then from birth
You let man go astray and fall.
You leave him then to suffer, for all
Guilt is requited here on earth.)
        (Goethe: *Wilhelm Meisters Lehrjahre*, bk II, chapter 13)

† Faust: *das ist der Weisheit letzter Schluss:*
        nur der verdient sich Freiheit wie das Leben
        der täglich sie erobern muss.

(The last result of wisdom stamps it true:
He only earns his freedom and existence
Who daily conquers them anew.) (Bayard Taylor)

§ Angels: *Wer immer strebend sich bemüht*
        den können wir erlösen!

(Whoe'er aspires unweariedly
Is not beyond redeeming!) (Bayard Taylor)

reason; nor human, for It had no understanding; nor devilish, for It was beneficent; nor angelic, for It often betrayed a malicious pleasure. It resembled chance, for It evinced no succession; it was like Providence for It hinted at connexion. It seemed to penetrate all that limits us . . . To this principle, which seemed to come in between all other principles and yet link them together, I gave the name of *the Daemonic*.[4]

Goethe's poetry had an immense influence on professional philosophy, and to this we must now return. It may however be remarked at this stage that, important as is Herder's discussion of culture, Kant was right in maintaining that neither morality nor religion can be understood simply as branches or spheres of culture – although it is equally true that they cannot be understood apart from an understanding of differences of culture and cultural change.

3

From Enlightenment to Romanticism: German Idealism

The movement of German thought from Fichte to Hegel which is generally called 'German Idealism' has no parallel in any of the other countries of Europe. And yet these writers were in constant contact with leading French and English personalities, and familiar with their works, so that we should try to see this German movement in its context of the development of European thought. And for this purpose 'Romanticism', a hopelessly inexact concept, serves nevertheless a useful purpose.

The changes generally grouped together as signifying the rise of Romanticism are of two kinds. In the first place there is a general widening of men's interests and a diminished concern with mathematics and physical science. Accounts of journeys in remote parts of the world became enormously popular, bringing a new interest in the philosophies of India and China, in the behaviour of primitive tribes and of strange animals. Another phenomenon, noticeable after about 1760, is the taste for the Satanic, the world as essentially evil, and for what the French call 'sombre' or black literature, in which meditations on death play a great part; Young's 'Night Thoughts' and Grey's 'Elegy in a Country Church-yard' become very popular on the continent. Along with interest in the primitive goes interest in simple, rustic life and in old folk-tales, represented in England by Ossian, in Germany by the Brothers Grimm and by A. W. Schlegel's praise of the *Nibelungenlied* as perhaps greater than the *Iliad* or the *Odyssey*. Finally, we find everywhere a revived interest in those periods of their country's history which had hitherto been neglected as barbarous – the Middle Ages.

But in this case differences in contemporary conditions caused a notable difference in the attitude towards the medieval manifested in the different European countries. For in England the Anglican Church had as good as abandoned all attempts to repress freedom of thought, and Roman Catholicism was almost non-existent. By contrast, in France, in spite of the divergence between strict law and actual practice, the legal power of the Church was formidable right up to the time of the Revolution; well-known works of atheistic writers got published and circulated, but they had to exercise ingenuity and caution; so that any rapprochement between philosophy and the Church would have been unthinkable. But in Germany the Lutheran and Calvinist Church authorities exercised a pressure which varied in the different states, and on the whole was not very severe. It did not prevent many philosophers from taking a positive attitude towards the Church and an interest in its doctrines and symbolisms, Catholic as well as Protestant; nor the conversion to Catholicism of notable writers such as Friedrich Schlegel. These new interests of cultivated society made their mark upon the work of Schelling and Hegel, and indeed of Goethe, who employs 'romantic' symbolisms while in general averse to all that the movement stood for. Goethe, an exception to most rules, an admirer of Byron, was fundamentally an 'enlightener', and against Romanticism, which he called 'the sickly' (*'das Kranke'*).

The second great change derives from growing awareness of the chameleon-like nature of the concept of reason, the fundamental concept of the Enlightenment. Here again the change took a different form in France and Britain on the one hand and in Germany on the other. In France Rousseau consciously proclaimed the superiority of sentiment to reason and initiated a new type of philosophy in reaction from rationalism, from about 1760 onwards. His *Emile* and above all his *Nouvelle Héloïse* had an immense popularity; they exalted not merely sentiment, but 'sentimental virtue' at the expense of reason. In Britain I think the cult of sentimentality did not take on to quite the same extent, in spite of Hutcheson's philosophy and Hume's famous dictum that 'reason both is and ought to be only the slave of the passions.'[1]

In Germany the development was strikingly different. Kant was greatly affected by Rousseau's conception of freedom, and freedom was a watchword of the pre-Romantic 'storm and stress' school of writers in Germany; but to set sentiment and instinct above reason is about the last thing that would have occurred to Kant. To a certain extent the difference of development in Germany may be explained by a difference in language; Germany has two words for reason, *Verstand* and *Vernunft*, and whereas in French *la raison* is always opposed to passions or sentiments, Kant opposes *Vernunft* to *Verstand* – the latter being a more purely mechanical type of reasoning, which merely connects given concepts in a logically correct manner. This usage is followed by all the German Idealists. *Vernunft* in the end signifies that which allows us to call almost any activity rational or reasonable. To the German it seems in no way a misuse of language to speak of practical reason imposing a rule upon our instincts in morality, or as operating on our senses to produce works of art. In both of these we recognize reasoning as a human activity; just how big a part it plays is a question.

But going beyond this, it became customary with the Idealists – and does not seem too far-fetched – to speak of rational sequences in nature and in history, namely those which seem readily intelligible to us as opposed to events that appear to be random in nature, or accidental in history. Such in nature are regular co-existences such as the colours of the spectrum or regular transformations such as water into steam into water. In history we find similarities of motive producing similar results, and also sequences that can be arranged in an order which seems intelligible to us, such as the recognized types of economy or types of political constitution. Again, it is not absurd to speak of 'reasoning' in the way a Michelangelo looks at his block of marble when starting

– what the Idealists called 'reason-in-intuition' (*Anschauung*, lit. 'looking'). So in the Idealists after Kant, reason becomes identified with 'order' that at first sight is purely natural or historical – like the Stoic *Logos* or the Neoplatonic *Nous*. Finally, for this cosmic reason Schelling substitutes the term 'the absolute'; and Hegel makes reason 'consciousness of the historical process' or even, ultimately, 'its becoming self-conscious in us'. The Germans in general never set sensibility above reason, as did the French.

All this may be decried as a metaphysics that is simply based on the misuse of a word. No doubt we need to be a lot more cautious than the Idealists were; no doubt the primary or paradigmatic use of the word is the reasoning we employ in deduction. Even that is more than the logic of strict entailment. But it does not seem an abuse to speak of reasoning about the suitability of scarce means to ends, or even reasoning about the relative importance of different ends within a projected whole, such as a town-plan. It is reasoning when I decide that the outcome of p will almost certainly be q (unwelcome) and yet I try p. Again one may speak of probabilistic reasoning, of which I believe there are a number of different kinds which should be distinguished, some susceptible of arithmetical treatment, some not. Again, there is reasoning which is appropriate to special fields, like the 'argument from silence' in history. Nor is mathematical reasoning, so far as I can judge, altogether equivalent to deductive logic. Again, there is 'modal' reasoning relative to values, turning upon 'must', 'must-not', 'may'. It does not seem an abuse to speak of the 'unconscious reasoning' of a scientist making his observations, or a person who has to make vital choices within a split second. 'Reason' primarily means 'human reasoning' and we should be aware that we are using it analogically in speaking, say, of the rational adaptation of animals to their environment, or of the digestive system. Yet it naturally occurs to us to speak in these ways.

German Idealism, child of the European Enlightenment, seeks to crown its achievement by discovering reason in unexpected quarters, and by attempting to link its different manifestations together. Fichte, with his deductive method, and the earlier Schelling are the ones guilty of the greatest abuse of the word 'reason'. Fichte is also guilty of a great abuse of the word *Ich* or *Ego*; it is surely nonsensical play with the word to assert that the Ego produces everything there is. In this he set the fashion for much Romantic literature.

To a greater extent than we find in the other countries, German Idealism takes seriously the active aspects of man, especially, but not only, as manifested in his moral choices. It regards morality not merely as exhibiting virtuous sentiments, nor as Hume's prevalence of 'calm pleasure'.[2] In this it is surely right. Again, it was surely right, with Schelling, for philosophy to seek to explore the significance of symbolism and mythology, for there is something akin to reason, even in fairy-stories, which controls their construction and makes them memorable. Following Montesquieu and perhaps Vico, the Idealists did much to explore the rational and irrational factors in history and in social institutions. Hegel above all, in exploring the various sorts of rational observation, production and action we undertake, and how they hang together, made a great and lasting contribution to human thought. His manner in the *Phenomenology* of displaying philosophy as a highly subjective and personal progress towards truth anticipates the later philosophy of Existentialism. Anyone who, like many others in our time, starts from common sense and tries to find a way through popular science, conventional religion, psychology, history, archaeology and anthropology, art and politics, to reach a vocation to which he can commit himself wholeheartedly, and a stable framework within which to assemble the current ideas and the suggested values poured out upon him by the mass-media – such a person must go through something like Hegel's sequence, and will find himself in many of the stages so oddly labelled by Hegel, such as 'unhappy consciousness', 'spiritual humbug and devotion to the cause', 'guilt and destiny'. The young may think they care for none of these things, but one observes them progressing from 'following one's heart' through a pop-aestheticism into contemplative religion, and perhaps (as especially in Holland) into committed politics.

The German Idealists and in particular Hegel saw the need of sophisticated man, who has got beyond the simple acceptance of given tradition (which Descartes had advocated), for a systematic framework of concepts that will help him to see the happenings of his individual life and of his times in perspective – in particular, to see how physical science, psychology and sociology can fit together; and how individual moral commitment can be made to fit in with economic and political activity. Hegel made a shot at this; he saw that it involved constantly going round a circle in thought, adapting one's concepts to the facts of nature and society, so as to get a truer view of their links. In our own time this sort of philosophy has been practised by Barbara Wootton, Michael Polanyi, Alasdair MacIntyre and Peter Winch among others (see Bibliography). It is the very kernel of the philosophical endeavour, at least in an epoch like our own, when the independent sciences, as well as other types of activity, such as games and communications, have each developed systems of concepts of their own.

In particular, German Idealism, especially if taken to include Lessing and Herder, should help us to get clear about the very complex relationships that obtain between culture, morality and religion. In one sense morality and religion are ingredients in a culture (*Kultur* = 'culture in the anthropological sense' denoting all the preferred habits and customs of a people or sub-cultural group – pubs, dowries, *Stammtische*, carnivals, pigeon-racing, flower-shows as well as art and literature). We cannot understand people's morals without understanding their culture. But in another sense, as the idealists emphasized, morality is on a different plane, and creative of much within a culture. Again morality is certainly not derived from religion, except in the external sense of being in part derived from the religious institutions of the culture. In another sense of the word, culture (*Bildung* – self-culture) is an important ingredient in a developed morality as it is in religion, and may give rise to what we can only call religious morality. Again, a certain religion may have little to do with morality and much with what one may call serious art. Again, Hegel's idea that there is a kinship between philosophy and religion is not absurd, although usually they are at daggers drawn; each claims to be in a certain sense authoritative. The contribution of the German Idealists to the clarification of these matters was considerable.

But their demerits were also great. They wrote far too much, partly owing to the German university system of piecework payment for lectures; and they wrote in a needlessly esoteric language. In consequence they are not much read outside of Germany. Worst of all, through misuse of the words 'ego' and 'self-consciousness' they frequently leave it obscure whether they are speaking about the individual person in his society or whether they are talking about some timeless absolute, an equivalent of God. The sort of philosophy which attributes all my thoughts, perceptions and actions to God is not very illuminating; but the sort which leaves it chronically in the dark (unlike, e.g. Shamanism) which ones are to be attributed to God and which to me is even less so. I think Fichte, Schelling and Hegel are all guilty of this, even when I think I know what they meant.

So ends the first round of German philosophy, inspired, one might say, by the great rationalistic urge of the Enlightenment, but coloured by the habits and modes of expression of Romanticism, with its desire for completeness and comprehensiveness.

4

German Idealism:
Fichte, Schelling and Hegel

As for Kant 'Philosophy' meant a rational criticism of all traditional beliefs, so for the German Idealists (it may be said), philosophy meant finding a hidden rational element in nature, in art, in social institutions. 'German Idealism' is the title generally given in Germany, and often elsewhere, to the work of the three philosophers Fichte, Schelling and Hegel, together with some specialists like Schleiermacher who wrote almost exclusively on religion – and, doubtfully, to the heretic Schopenhauer, whose thought starts from the same origin, though he violently attacked all the others. Of these philosophers Hegel is by far the most important, both for his own insights and for his subsequent influence; but his work is not clearly intelligible without some understanding of his contemporaries – who are in a sense his predecessors – Fichte and Schelling (though Schelling outlived him). They were all consciously and admittedly disciples of Kant, and for all their differences of personality represent a type of thought distinct both from what had gone before and what was to come after. They are all concerned to present above all a unitary view of the world (which, they considered, Kant had failed to do) through a sort of deification of reason and a great extension of this concept to include intuition and feeling, conscious and unconscious. This is what we should now call revisionary metaphysics, a deliberate shifting of the usual meaning of certain fundamental concepts.

This great change in the style of professional philosophy is obviously linked with the change in style of literature and art which we call the Romantic movement. Common to these philosophers and the Romantic writers such as the Schlegels, Tieck, Novalis, are a new interest in matters despised or neglected by the Enlightenment, such as folk-culture, medieval art and thought, mythology, oriental art and literature, mysticism such as that of Eckhart and Böhme, and Spinoza (hitherto almost unknown). But the influence of the Romantics must not be exaggerated; Fichte is in some ways an extreme rationalist; it is not at all true that Fichte or Hegel regarded philosophy as a kind of poetry. And conversely Fichte's central idea of the creative Ego was an important influence upon the later German Romantic poets.

Johann Gottlieb Fichte (1762–1814) is important chiefly as the originator of a new, very strange style in German philosophy. He was an enthusiast, much influenced by the French Revolution and the pre-Romanticism of *Sturm und Drang* ('storm and stress'), 'always something of a preacher', as appears in his very eloquent *Addresses to the German Nation*, his *Closed Commercial State* and in the very title of his work, the *Daylight-clear Statement, to Compel People to Understand the Truth*. He asked for the job of an official propagandist with the army, but was refused.

Fichte's overriding aim is to give a picture of the world as a whole based on the absolute primacy of the moral consciousness, a picture as indisputable as the logical tautologies from which he claims to deduce it. 'My world is the object and sphere of my duties and absolutely nothing else.' His main philosophical work is the *Wissenschaftslehre* (doctrine of science). He put out several versions of this, but they are all alike in the fantastic claim to deduce all the main features of the world from the logical tautologies: 'A is A' and 'not-A is not A', *plus* Kant's doctrine of the free moral self.[1] Apart from the self-assertion of the Ego, he argues, there is nothing; from this all else derives. (The word I have translated 'assertion' (conventionally translated 'positing') *setzen*, means literally 'to put down', 'set down', 'take as existing'.) His three supposed indubitable philosophical propositions in German are as follows:

Das Ich setzt sich.
Das Ich setzt das Nicht-Ich als Nicht Ich.
Das Nicht-Ich wird im Ich gesetzt.

('The Ego asserts itself as existing; the Ego asserts the non-Ego as not itself; the non-Ego is asserted within the Ego.') And, as motive force for this whole performance: *'Das Ich soll sich setzen als anschauend'* ('the Ego has a duty to assert itself as perceptive'). This he terms the dialectic of thesis, antithesis and synthesis, a device usually (but falsely) attributed to Hegel.[2] By this logical *tour de force* he proceeds to a sort of speculative psychology: 'Instinct [*Trieb*] must be asserted and defined . . . Feeling must be asserted and defined.' The Pure Ego, 'since its activity is unlimited, must unconsciously produce ideas in us . . . There must be an equilibrium between the strivings of the Ego and the counter-strivings of the non-Ego.' These are some specimens of the metaphysical psychology, of which the *Wissenschaftslehre* (by no means what we would expect of a theory of science) chiefly con-sists. 'Observe your self-assertings!' (*'Bemerke dein Selbstsetzen!'*) is a slogan of the new version of 1797. In this new style of philoso-phy the activity of the 'I', Ego or self is made responsible for everything that is or happens. But this leads to a split between the pure Ego and the actual conscious Ego; in the later versions the pure Ego becomes more and more unknowable, like Schelling's absolute, and more and more identified with God. In his *Instruc-tion for a Blessed Life* this identification is complete: 'the Divine becomes manifest in us.' Although his is a religion of moral fervour, his work on morals, *Sittenlehre* (1798), does not take us much beyond the ideas of Kant. He divides duties into (1) general unconditional duties – to respect the formal freedom of others; (2) general conditioned duties – never to let your body be an object of enjoyment, but to perfect it for the glory of God; (3) particular vocational duties – those of spouses, parents, scholars, teachers, officials and of the lower classes, whose vocation is to work for and respect the higher. He states the supreme principle of morality as 'Act always in accordance with your best belief about duty, or in accordance with your conscience.' Evil consists only in laxity and laziness which lead first to cowardice and then to falseness.

Schiller, Fichte's fellow-professor at Jena, with whom he had much in common, thought him more rigorous in his manner of life than Kant. Like Schelling, he advocated asceticism, as 'a perpetual reminder of duty'. He seems however to have been popular and to have effected as pro-Rector useful reforms in connection with the duelling and drinking customs of the students' corporations, until he was forced to leave Jena on being charged with atheism. It seems surprising both that he should have been so charged and that Goethe should not have been able to save him; it is likely that his political ideas and his unbending manners may have had something to do with it. For he was an odd character; Jaspers describes him as being fanatical, barbaric, sensationalistic, not very honest or truthful. After a short stay in Königsberg, he spent the rest of his life in Berlin.

He initiated a new deductive style of philosophy, but one which I think does not have much appeal to our generation. It just seems an inconvenient misuse of language to assert that 'I' in any sense *produce* the world, or that whenever I act morally it is God acting in me.

Friedrich Wilhelm Joseph von Schelling (1775–1854) was the philosopher whose affinity with the writers constituting the Romantic movement is the most lasting and the deepest. He went to Tübingen, from a more cultured home than that of Kant and Fichte, at the age of fifteen, and there he met Hegel and the poet, Hölderlin, whose intimate friend he became. In 1798 he was appointed at a very early age Professor at Jena, owing to the influence of Goethe, who thought he saw a kindred spirit in the author of *Ideen zu einer Philosophie der Natur*, published in the previous year. There he met the Schlegels, and married Caroline, August Schlegel's divorced wife, with whom he was very happy; this seems in no way to have impaired his friendship with the Schlegel brothers, the arch-Romantics. He remained in Jena till

1827, when he was called to Munich and was active there as professor until 1841. Like Fichte he had a sense of vocation (*Sendungsbewusstsein*); but it took him in a quite a different direction.

In the course of a long life Schelling wrote a great deal, and his work shows considerable changes and developments in his thought. Yet through it all we can discern certain trends. Unlike Fichte he showed little interest in questions of morality or politics; and for him history is a story of cultural rather than of political change. As Fichte may be said to start from the *Critique of Practical Reason*, so Schelling's philosophy originates in Kant's third critique, the *Critique of Judgement*, which exhibits reason as operative in art, culture and the science of organic life. With Schelling it is the objective world, not that of individual psychology, which we must examine to find traces of reason. This reason, he thinks, should rather be termed the 'absolute', since it is in perception, contemplation, and artistic effort that it is to be discerned, rather than in logic or abstract reflection. Fichte's pure Ego, he says, is just a postulate, which we use to explain the affinities to our human selves which we find in nature, in art, and finally in mythology and religion.

In his *First Draft of a System of Natural Philosophy*, Schelling says that we must recognize that intelligence is unconsciously productive in the world of our perception, just as it is consciously productive in the creation of the idea world. There is kinship between nature and art, such that art makes us aware of features of nature we would otherwise have failed to realize. In a sense too, science is a kind of artistic construction, guided by ideals of order of which we are only half-conscious until they find expression. This to his mind justifies speculation about the different forces in nature – fanciful though his talk about, e.g. 'absolute fluidity' and 'absolute activity' seems to us. His natural philosophy is not of much interest nowadays, though for the historian of science it is important to discover the concepts which were available to science in a certain culture at a certain stage of its development, and their necessary interrelations.

His *Transzendentalphilosophie* (1800) may be regarded as a Fichtean interlude, also attempting to deduce everything from the tautology

'A is A' and the Ego. But for him the chief characteristic of the Ego is productive intuition, from which he deduces our concept of matter and our concept of the work of art – the latter resulting from the productive intuition of genius, a favourite idea with the Romantics. Art, far more than science, is capable of revealing the individual to himself, so that he can know himself objectively. In all this however it is *'Ein Geist der in allem dichtet'* – 'One Spirit which is the universal creative poet in everything.' Already in the *Philosophy of Art* (1802), he claims that it is the work of art, rather than philosophy of practical activity, which alone can manifest the 'identity of the conscious and the unconscious in the absolute', which alone combines the ideal and the given. And there is a kind of art which is of special significance, providing both the subject-matter of important art-works and the material of philosophy – symbolic and mythological art; about this he has a great deal more to say in the final stage of his philosophy.

Meantime he wrote the *System der Philosophie* (1801), generally reckoned as the second stage in the development of his thought. Influenced by his discovery of Indian thought, he maintains the complete identity of thought and nature in an absolute which is unknowable and the original ground (*Urgrund*, akin to Böhme's concept of the *'Ungrund'* (lit. 'primordial ground') for the ultimate being). About this nothing can be said; it is as Hegel so unkindly called it, 'the night in which all cows are black'! Schelling praised contemplation without really practising it. He was essentially a gnostic, with a love for the esoteric and exotic.

The latest stage of his thought, to be found in his posthumously published works, *Philosophie der Mythologie* and *Philosophie der Offenbarung*, is of much greater interest. Given the absolute unknowability of the absolute, he raises the disturbing question, why is there anything at all? why not nothing? – a question central to some of the existentialist philosophy of our time. Schelling's answer is to give a metaphysical view of history, as an emergence of different societies, each with its own mythology and religion. History displays 'the evolution of the divine principle in history'. It starts when 'God alienates himself from himself'. This is the cause of the fall of man as depicted in Genesis or in the ever-worsening gold, silver, bronze and iron ages of Hesiod. All peoples have their own appropriate mythology, their own imaginative description of powers of nature, heroes, spirits, gods. This he holds is a fundamental fact for any understanding of art and of religion.

A comparison of mythologies leads Schelling to think that we can discover some necessary, *a priori* features about their relationship. A genuine myth can never be just the invention of a certain individual at a certain time. But we should not say either that myths are the invention of a certain people or tribe, for a people or tribe as a unit is to a great extent the creation of its myths. It is a process 'out of which theologies, peoples and languages arise in a lawful order'. He calls it the *'theogonic'* – God-creating – process. All mythology is an imaginative amalgamation of the ideal and the given; it is indispensable for man.

But the proportions of these two elements are found to vary in the different mythologies, for instance in the Indian and the Greek, the Hebrew–Christian and the Nordic. For us, he claims, the most important difference is the difference between the Greek mythology and the Judaic–Christian; the former is an idealization of natural forces, the latter of human social life in history. In all mythology both elements are to be found, but, he says, the one is explicit, the other veiled or hidden. The Judaic-Christian tradition, in which a mythology of history – myths of fall, reformation, reverses, salvation by a Messiah, apocalyptic glory and happiness – predominates, he distinguishes from the other, pagan, mythology as 'revelation'. Revealed religion is to be distinguished from other religion merely as the second stage of the process; it is 'the second form of real religion that is independent of reason'. All real religion contains the same elements. (The third form is 'philosophical religion, which is a final goal, but it does not yet exist'.)

Not only a people's art-forms, but also its language, are influenced by its mythologies; indeed we can see that all these three elements of culture influence each other, and that we should not always ascribe priority to language. It would take us beyond the scope of this introductory work to examine Schelling's detailed interpretation of the Christian mythology in his *Monotheismus*, subtitled the 'Special part of the Philosophy of Revelation'. He thinks it a characteristic of Christianity that the symbolical prevails over the allegorical. 'The Christian Church is to be seen as a work of art.' Schelling fancied himself as founder of a 'third religion', but without any real understanding of what such a task implied.

Our much greater knowledge of the variety of mythologies available throughout the world makes it far more difficult for us to discern any lawful order in them. Yet we are inclined to allow some connections between available language, available art-forms, available stories or motifs (iconography), even if we are not clear just what they are. Genius utilizes them in ways that astonish and illuminate, but even genius can never wholly transcend these limits of what is available at the time. In recent times Ernst Cassirer and his pupil Suzanne Langer have greatly developed this type of philosophy.

Georg Wilhelm Friedrich Hegel (1770–1831) was the son of a minor fiscal official at Stuttgart, Württemberg. As a bright boy, he was sent at the early age of fifteen to the endowed school (*Stift*) of Tübingen, a grammar school with a religious bias. From there he went on to study at the University. There he met the great classical poet, Hölderlin, who became his dearest friend, until Hölderlin's madness, which overcame him in his thirties. Hegel's major writings exhibit, it may be said, the professorial style at its worst; but as his letters and occasional pieces show, he was quite capable of writing clearly and well, and wrote quite decent poetry on occasion. He was sought after as an agreeable social companion, especially in his earlier years, and his life was by no means one of untroubled absorption in academic affairs. He had an illegitimate son whom he persuaded his wife to accept and bring up as her son; a period of poverty, which took him to Switzerland as a house-tutor; a later uncongenial period as headmaster of a grammar school at Nuremberg; and a life much disturbed by the marchings and counter-marchings of French troops of occupation about his country – as in the well-known story that he completed his first major work, the *Phenomenology*, to the sound of the guns of the battle of Jena. He was nineteen at the time of the French

Revolution and was greatly moved by the world events through which he lived; a sense of vital movement and change animates his work, and makes it for us, who live in the same sort of epoch, worth exerting some effort to penetrate his obscurities.

Yet we learn from his contemporaries that he was a thoroughly bad lecturer, feeling himself obliged by his position to cultivate a professorial style, and by his own native temperament to cram in a great deal of material, as it occurred to him on the spur of the moment. He would keep on faltering and stopping, as if to search for the truth (a manner of lecturing not unlike that ascribed to Wittgenstein in our own day) – and in the end those students who persisted in attending generally caught the feeling that this search was of supreme importance. But we hear that he sometimes had an audience of no more than four, and only on one special occasion did it reach a hundred. Only after some doubts did Goethe decide to appoint him to the professorship of philosophy at Jena in 1801. The style of his works makes the present author's task, of trying to give a faithful account free from technicalities and disputes about interpretation, peculiarly difficult.

At Jena Hegel had the opportunity of meeting Schiller, a fellow Swabian, who we know had already influenced him considerably through his *Letters on Aesthetic Education* (1795). In these Schiller makes art, and especially poetry, the resultant of the combination or synthesis of two rival drives, *Spieltrieb* (play-urge) and *Form-trieb* (urge towards form or order). Hegel shared Schiller's aim to overcome the Kantian gulf set between science and art on the one hand, and moral life on the other. Both men employ the concept of *Geist* or *spirit*, as a creative force manifesting itself not merely in the conciousness of the individual. This becomes a central concept of the new, idealistic, philosophy. Hegel never became intimate with Goethe, but the appearance of *Faust, ein Fragment* (the first incomplete published version of Goethe's great drama) certainly influenced his *Phenomenology*. His philosophy may be said to show a decided spiritual affinity with the Goethe of *Faust* and of *Wilhelm Meister*. Goethe greatly respected Hegel, though confessing that he did not understand him. Hegel was a child of the Enlightenment and so was deeply interested in religion, which is the subject of his early works (only recently published and now mostly translated into English). Like Schiller, he contrasted Christianity unfavourably with the life-affirming religion of the Greeks. This was no novelty at the time, but Hegel was the first person, as far as is known, actually to criticize the character of Jesus, contrasting him unfavourably with Socrates. It may be thought that this is inconsistent with Hegel's later attitude to Christianity and Hellenism, in the third part of the *Encyclopaedia*, the *Philosophy of Spirit*; but there Christianity is treated merely as a step towards philosophy, which is to include and supersede it. Both Schiller and Hegel hoped for the restoration of the wholeness of man; but that which Schiller had hoped would come through art, Hegel hoped for from philosophy – in the spirit of the late Greco–Roman philosophers such as Plotinus and Julian.

Before turning to his individual works, it is worth saying something about the character of Hegel's philosophy as a whole, and particularly about what it is not. He has been most unlucky in his disciples; but he would not have had so many and various disciples were it not for a many-sided richness to be found in his work – something appealing to such very different men as Feuerbach, Marx, Royce, Bradley, McTaggart, Croce, Hippolyte and Sartre. One popular error must be countered at the start; recent scholarship has made it perfectly clear that he was not a panlogicist like Fichte, claiming to deduce facts from a few self-evident propositions by means of a new dialectical logic. Nor did he ever maintain, with Bradley and McTaggart, that time is unreal; our conceptions of time may be shifting and fluid, but development in time is the heart of his system. Mystical absorption in the absolute by mere feeling, as preached in England by Bradley, is quite remote from his thought. Equally remote is Marx's or Engels's idea of dialectic as a method of predicting facts. He uses the word 'dialectic' seldom. The frequent, though not invariable, arrangement of his chapters in triads or groups of three is a method of arrangement, not a picture of the world; as a rule there is no question of the first two being combined and superseded in the third.

He does indeed believe that there is a supremely important element of reason, of intelligibility, to be discovered both in the course of nature and in the course of history, and that it is the business of philosophy to make this clear, by research into transitions and connections and our ways of thinking about them. He ridicules Professor Krug's demand that he should deduce the existence of his pen, but claims that we can in a sense give a reason for the existence of iron, given all the other features we know of the periodic table of elements; or again for wars to acquire iron, given its superiority for weapons over other metals. Such is reason in the philosophy of nature and in the philosophy of history. Some of the misunderstanding arises from his inconvenient use of the word 'necessary' to mean not 'logically necessary', but the opposite of accidental or capricious. Marx's idea of the deducible inevitability of Communism finds no justification in Hegel.

Finally, there is the widespread error that Hegel regarded his own as the final philosophy, in which the absolute becomes completely conscious of itself. He is perfectly clear on this point: 'just so far has the world-spirit got up to now'; 'the present standpoint of philosophy is as follows . . .'; 'no philosophy can transcend its own epoch'; 'the series of spiritual formations is for the present concluded with this'.[3]

The General Character of his Philosophy; His Personal Pilgrimage; His Final System

Like all the great Germans with whom we have been concerned, Hegel believed he could give his readers a whole system of concepts which would show up the hidden connections in things. Its novelty lay in a certain summing-up of previous systems by setting them in a new light. The history of philosophy was not for him just a series of errors, in spite of the many accidental factors about it, such as the premature death of one writer, the loss of a manuscript, a mistranslation from one language to another; it is 'the result of the exertions of the spirit for almost 2,500 years'. This new conception of the history of philosophy he attempts to set forth in the preface to his first main work, the *Phenomenology of Spirit*. But in this preface the reader is brought up against Hegel at his most obscure; I find myself unable to agree with those who have found it 'one of the greatest philosophical undertakings of all time' (Marcuse) or 'a literary as well as a philosophical master-piece' (Findlay). The original does achieve a certain grandeur of style, and has many a striking phrase but also many an obscure paragraph. I have decided to leave the reader to judge these apprais-als, either in the original text or the very careful translation of Walter Kaufmann, and to content myself with a mere summary of its principal points.

A genuine philosophy, Hegel maintains, must be first scientific, i.e. a rational system (in the European sense of science, not the restricted English sense of 'natural science' only); this means that the concepts it employs, and their relations, must be clearly analysed. It must not build on a few propositions that someone finds intuitively true; it cannot be a matter of common sense; it requires penetration into a system of thinking. Moreover in philosophy the true must take up and include, and by including supersede (aufheben) the false propositions of former thinkers, making clear why they seemed formerly satisfactory and now seem inadequate. For the true is the whole; a proposition can only be judged when seen in its place. He contrasts philosophy with mathematics in this respect.

Finally, he writes, we must see the true, 'not as substance but as subject' – a very obscure phrase meaning, I think, that it should be spirit as living and growing, at first in the progression of the individual consciousness from mere sense-certainty to science, but also to a further scientific or moral certainty going far beyond the individual consciousness and permeating society. We are to follow its growth from simple sense-certainty of fact to the heights of law, art and religion. These are plainly inter-individual or super-personal. The word 'phenomenology', taken over from Kant, means roughly an extension of psychology to embrace this super-individual sphere of society or culture.

The two versions of Hegel's philosophy

But I think it is a good deal easier to discover the character of Hegel's system from his work rather than from this programmatic preface. Indeed he begins with an assertion like Wittgenstein; philosophy is what philosophers have done, no more and no less. The trouble for an expositor is that he set forth his philosophy in two different forms, each with its own drawbacks. The first form, that of the *Phenomenology*, is certainly not very systematic – indeed, it has been described by Kaufmann as a 'series of skits, tableaux and orations', and by Hegel himself as a Bacchanalian orgy. The second form, that of the *Encyclopaedia*, is indeed systematic, but was written as a compendium or basis for lectures, intended to be supplemented by the spoken word. One must attempt to do justice to both versions of his thought. In fact what we have is a compendium, the *Encyclopaedia*, supplemented by the *Philosophy of Right* and the *Science of Logic* published in his lifetime, and by the *Philosophy of History*, *Lectures on the History of Philosophy* and *Philosophy of Fine Art* published on the basis of students' notes after his death. These latter contain some of his most interesting work, adulterated however by pupils.

1. *The phenomenology of spirit: Hegel's personal pilgrimage*
The *Phenomenology* more than the other works betrays the rather odd way Hegel's mind worked. The theme of this work is the progression of a mind from the simplest certainties of sense and common sense to more broadly-based certainties of science, law, morals and religion. The first section moves from simple sense-judgements to discussion of why we have illusions; and then to the popular-science view of the world which thinks of, e.g. this table as *really* a collection of particles and empty space (Eddington's famous remark).

Then comes the transition to the second section, entitled 'Self-Consciousness' – over against my fellows. (Unlike the English word, the German word so translated has a nuance of 'self-assurance'.) This section starts with the famous discussion of the relation of master and slave. It certainly seems odd that this should be regarded as the primary human relationship, but perhaps a candid view of history might justify Hegel. He rightly sees that in this relationship each party falls short of being fully a person, and that each can suffer when he realizes this – the slave too can feel superior (*selbstbewusst*) in realizing his master's utter dependence on him. His labour may be a far more genuine conquest of material necessity than the mere plans of the master. Now Hegel holds that in both parties this relationship gives rise to an acute consciousness of man's freedom, thwarted though that may be. So from this we pass on, by fairly intelligible if unexpected transitions, to '*Stoicism*' – freedom in spite of external circumstances, through control of one's desires; 'scepticism' – freedom from merely traditional prejudices and unexamined beliefs; and finally 'unhappy consciousness'. This is Hegel's odd term for the traditional Christian sense of guilt, in which man feels that because of his natural desires 'he cannot do the things that he would' (Paul) and yearns for a freedom which can be found only through supernatural salvation.

The third section is entitled 'reason'. In this self-consciousness is aware of, and glories in, its rationality. It begins with 'observational reason', which may be equated with the modern term 'scientism', unlimited confidence in our planned observation of nature and consciousness. (In dealing with the latter he amuses himself at the expense of two would-be scientific fashions of the time, physiognomy and phrenology.) But rationality is concerned with social activity also, not just with observation; so the next section, on social activity, deals with the life of consistent pleasure-seeking; then with the life of sentimental intuition, 'following one's heart' as he terms it; finally with another sort of sentimentality, which he oddly entitles 'virtue and the course of the world' (*Tugend und der Weltlauf*). By this I think he means a lack of seriousness or realism, indicating the man who says to himself: do what is considered the proper thing and don't bother about the consequences, and all will be well – but all is *not* well! The next sort of false sentimentality has the oddest title of all, 'spiritual fauna and humbug', or, 'devotion to the cause', which is the sort of humbug which we might label escapist commitment to any cause that comes along, to escape from self-awareness. This is a caricature of the true way of finding causes to which one can commit oneself. That is described in the next two sections; the first about taking traditional maxims as guides and the second about testing them. This leads on to the next main section, the life of inter-personal institutions and customs, which he later called 'objectified spirit'.

From this point the work consists of what we might call a psychology of different possible attitudes that can be taken to the social institutions within which we all live and move. It is of interest to see how Hegel now pursues this theme; but it must be borne in mind that this, the most characteristic part of his system, was treated by him more fully later on. From this point therefore we shall trace only very briefly the path he followed in his personal pilgrimage rather than the substance of his teaching. He considers in the first subsection customary morality, with special emphasis on the relation between man and women, which often gives rise to acute questions about what is due to divine or natural law, what to merely human and local law. This leads him on to questions of guilt and destiny, which we are compelled to face in sex-relations more than anywhere else. We may then look, but often vainly, to legal status, to solve our problems; this cannot be ignored, but is often felt to be but a blind and fumbling guide. Such self-questioning, perhaps owing to his own sex-relations, brings Hegel to the famous sub-section entitled: 'The Self-estranged Spirit, Self-Culture' (*'Der Selbsentfremdete Geist, Bildung'*). The word 'self-estrangement' or 'alienation from one's true self' will play, as we shall see, a major role in the thought of the young Marx; here, as far as I know, it occurs for the first time.

Bildung (self-improvement) was a fashionable ideal of the times, especially since Goethe's education-novel (*Bildungsroman*), *Wilhelm Meister*, and Hegel is here much concerned with conditions of his own time. But much is relevant to ours – to the boundless faith, earlier this century, in the regenerative power of education, and our more recent scepticism about this. The apparent value attached by his society to culture may, thinks Hegel, be illusory; the individual's claim to culture may be just a by-product of the struggle for wealth or power. The conspicuous zeal of Weimar for culture in the sense of self-improvement was a noble product of the great European movement we call the 'Enlightenment', a struggle for truth against superstition.

But the Enlightenment of the French *philosophes* in Hegel's view often had one of two unfortunate results. Either it ended in a rigid-religious, persecuting creed such as that of Robespierre's 'supreme being'; or else, worse, in absolute emancipation from all respect for all laws and traditions rooted in the past and from all social bonds. And so he concludes with a description of 'Absolute Freedom and Terror' – the freedom of the *acte gratuit* (Gide) – the wholly senseless act done just to show that you are free to do it, to show how free you are!*

This main section concludes with what we might call the perplexities of the moral conscience when faced with the realities of social life: 'Moralism'; 'Moral Duplicity'; 'Conscience and the "Beautiful Soul"'; 'Evil and Forgiveness'. I think his treatment is less satisfactory here than in his later works; he almost seems to say that the man who aims to act morally *must* end up either in aestheticism – the cult of the beautiful soul – or in religion.

The *Phenomenology* concludes with what he was later to call 'spirit absolute': natural religion, the religion of art, revealed religion (Christianity) and finally absolute knowledge (philosophy). Art is here treated as a kind of religion which has its being in statues and pictures, and gives rise to a tension between love of the beautiful and consciousness of absolute demands, among them to a demand for a revealed religion of a divine individual. Finally, in those who are conscious of the absolute, present in this divine individual in the form of love, there may arise an absolute knowledge. 'In this ultimate form of spirit, the spirit . . . knows itself conceptually.' It knows itself in and through the exercise of a self-conscious person re-thinking all he has ever thought in the many stages of the pilgrimage which he has just described – and ideally, in a sense, by re-thinking what mankind has hitherto thought, so far as that is possible for a certain individual living at a certain time. A sort of old age of the spirit, recollecting in tranquillity the stages it has gone through.

Hegel's *Phenomenology* was certainly a novel way of presenting a philosophy; the only works I can think of at all resembling it are Boethius's *Consolation of Philosophy* and Nietzsche's *Zarathustra*.

* Cf. André Gide, *Les Caves du Vatican* (London 1961).

Unfortunately, it utilizes a great deal of professorial language, but it is really a highly personal, unacademic work. As can be seen from such sections as 'The Unhappy Consciousness', 'Spiritual Fauna and Humbug', 'The Self-estranged Spirit', 'Moral Duplicity', 'Absolute Freedom and Terror', it represents Hegel's highly individual pilgrimage from a dissatisfaction with Christianity, Kantian morality and revolutionary enthusiasm, to a rather new kind of rationalism arising out of and tinged with religion. It seems to have been begun during the unhappy time when he was headmaster of the secondary school at Nuremberg. It includes much which had not been thought proper to philosophy hitherto. It is most difficult to read, but apart from its interest as an autobiographical document it suggests connections between many items of experience which we are accustomed to hold apart, and fresh insights, for example, into many different types of sentimentality and *mauvaise foi*.

The *Phenomenology* represents Hegel's progress to an acceptance of life with all its ills, because life is productive of rational social order, aesthetic religion (religious art) and philosophy. This was to be a central theme for his successors, Schopenhauer and Nietzsche, who are often said to have initiated life-philosophy.

2. Hegel's final system: 'The Encyclopaedia of the Philosophical Sciences'

In line with the purpose of the present work, I intend to pass over the ponderous first part, the *Science of Logic*, extremely lightly. Hegel himself describes it in the introduction: 'the system of logic is the realm of shadows' the world of essences, freed from all sensuous concreteness. Work in this realm of shadows is the absolute discipline of consciousness. In Findlay's words, 'In it he recommends a certain way of talking about the world, discovers flaws and inadequacies in it, then supersedes it . . . until his last recommendation supersedes and comprehends all others.'[4] Prior to 1914 it was generally considered Hegel's greatest work, and volumes have been written about it. It was viewed as the scaffolding which he first erected in order to build up in it his philosophy of spirit – a false view, I think.

The *Logic* examines the very general concepts which we may, and to some extent must, employ: being, becoming, being-here-and-now (*Dasein*), quantity, number, measure; then essence, identity, difference, opposition and contradiction, ground for . . . (or condition of . . .); then existence and the apparent; whole and parts; force and its manifestation; and the 'absolute relationships' of substantiality, causality and reciprocal interaction. (It concludes with two sections which do not altogether fit in with the general tenor of the work.) In the main it is an exhibition of the way these very general concepts – 'categories' – grow out of one another and *shift their meaning according to what is contrasted with them*; of this we must be aware if we are to achieve a connected view of life – what he sometimes calls 'the concept', also 'the absolute idea' (as goal) – a world-view freed from mere caprice and the merely-accidental elements in one person's particular experience. Much of the earlier part is directed against his predecessors, who took as their basic concepts such concepts as 'being', 'monad', 'thing-in-itself' without sufficient awareness of their slipperiness, their variation in meaning. He certainly does *not* undertake the conjuring trick that has been attributed to him – of deducing the nature of the absolute from 'being', 'nothing' and 'becoming', by means of a new logic that permits contradictions. It may be noted that the absolute is here abandoned as a category; and that the ultimate form of thought is called 'the concept' (also translated, but inconveniently, as 'the notion'). What he says about it is certainly very obscure, but he tells us it is the state of 'a self that penetrates the object by thinking; . . . as it was in intuitive and picture-thinking, the object was but appearance'.

The *Logic* is full of interesting footnotes. It is certainly not of any value as a textbook of logic, and its contents would probably be labelled 'semantics' today. It is of interest to anyone who wants to answer the question: what is philosophy? on the basis of the works acknowledged philosophers have written – as Hegel himself did – and so is obliged to examine carefully the abstract conceptual counters they work with.

The general character of the *Encyclopaedia* is well described in the introduction to the *History of Philosophy*:

The courage for truth, faith in the powers of Spirit is the first condition of philosophy. Man since he is spirit can and should deem himself worthy of the highest. The initially-concealed or locked-up appearance of the universe has no strength to resist his courage to know. The history of philosophy represents the noble spirits who by the boldness of their reasoning penetrated into the nature of things, of man and of God, unveiling its depth for us ... And yet people who consider themselves able to express the matter with more thorough judgement call this history a gallery of follies or at least of aberrations ... Truth however is one; the instinct of reason has this insuperable feeling of faith ... But this proposition, that truth is only one, is itself abstract and false ... Only the living, that which is spirit, moves and stirs essentially, and develops ... Philosophy is for itself the recognition of this development, it is itself this thinking development ... Thus philosophy is system in the process of development.[5]

The three main divisions of the *Encyclopaedia* are entitled *Logic*; *Philosophy of Nature*; *Philosophy of Spirit*. The main divisions of the latter, most important, part are entitled 'Subjective Spirit'; 'Objective Spirit'; and 'Absolute Spirit'. As the contents of the first of these parts have been largely discussed already in connection with the *Phenomenology* and the *Logic*, we shall concentrate upon the last part of the system, which on the whole has still the most interest for our own time.* These are sketched in the *Encyclopaedia*, and amplified as has been explained in the *Philosophy of Right*, the *Philosophy of History*, the *Philosophy of Art* and the *History of Philosophy*. As a guide to the way Hegel saw his system, I reproduce here W. Kaufmann's most illuminating diagram (reprinted from *Hegel* by permission of Doubleday & Company, Inc.)

Hegel's system is a circle which he recognizes will have to be gone over and rectified again and again by subsequent philosophers. 'The Spirit is the Circle that returns into itself, presupposes the beginning and reaches it only in the end.' Only if one sees it as a circle can one make sense of the order of the constituent parts. As for the individual enquirer, one can, I believe, enter the circle at any of the points on the circumference, according to one's personal

* See Bibliography for new translation of this by Miller.

Sittlichkeit   Art

OBJECTIVE   ABSOLUTE

Moralität   Religion

SPIRIT   SPIRIT

Law   Philosophy

PHILOSOPHY OF SPIRIT

Psychology
            SUBJECTIVE   LOGIC
Phenomenology
            SPIRIT
Anthropology

PHILOSOPHY OF NATURE

interests or the social concerns of the age; but once bitten by the
spirit of philosophy one is constrained to go all round it. One cannot
say: I will only interest myself in the philosophy of law or of
natural science, I will keep off psychology or art. It was Hegel's
merit to see that – and to some extent how – these manifestations
of the human spirit are tied together, the individual with the social,
the contemplative with the active. Movement round the circle is
kept up through the mobility or elasticity of the concepts which we
are obliged to employ; e.g. the concept of cause in jurisprudence
leads us to compare it with the concept of cause in physical science;*
and the elasticity of the concepts is shown up both by considering
contrasted concepts (e.g. cause-chance, and cause-accidental); and
by considering marginal cases (e.g. should we term a virus 'alive'?).
This, I believe, is what Hegel is about in his often extremely
obscure statements about the universal leading us to the particular
and then to the individual which is seen to incorporate both. Though
not envisaging dialectic as a deductive process (as we have seen),
he does frequently use this language of 'universal', 'particular'
and 'individual'. Dialectic is an immanent progress, which shows
up the one-sidedness and limitations of our common concepts

* What F. Waismann called 'the open texture' of the concept.

as well as of our scientific concepts (*Verstandesbestimmungen*), and this is the motive force of scientific progress. It is certainly *one* of the major motive forces – the attempt to solve acute problems by radically revising the meaning hitherto given to a certain fundamental concept, such as 'heat', 'atom', 'simultaneity'.

Having already discussed the first part of the *Encyclopaedia* – what he calls logic – I propose to enter the circle at the point entitled 'philosophy of nature'. Many have scorned this section, described by Hegel as 'the idea resolving to go freely out of itself as nature', as *a priori* science, which is fundamentally absurd; nature cannot be spun out of our heads. Hegel is quite aware of this, of the element of pure contingency in nature, the element which in the light of all the laws we have been able to formulate looks like pure chance – e.g. mutations in the behaviour of individual chromosomes. He calls this 'the *powerlessness of reason*' as manifest in nature (*Ohnmacht der Vernunft*). Yet unless we assume some intelligible pattern, we should have nothing we could call 'nature'. We assume for example that mathematical reasoning will apply and go on applying to unobserved nature; we do not for a moment consider that perhaps from next January it may cease to apply – as Russell once suggested. To a certain extent we can consider the system of concepts which are employed in physics or biological science at any one time, and this may be a useful endeavour in modern histories of science; such is Hegel's philosophy of nature. But in all this to draw the line clearly between our tools of thought (no doubt suggested by the phenomena) and the phenomena themselves is a tricky business,* and Hegel certainly goes astray sometimes, as when he purports to show that Newton's view of light cannot be correct, or that there cannot be evolution of species. The work has been generally neglected, although recently re-habilitated by Petry.† Hegel's main point is that even observation is affected by our available concepts. Man needs the conception of nature as over against him, yet not totally unresponsive to his efforts to observe and comprehend – indeed as instructing him.

* Very clearly expounded in Braithwaite's *Scientific Explanation*.
† *Hegel's Philosophy of Nature*.

The next section, 'subjective spirit', comprises the sub-sections 'Anthropology', which describes the soul as slumbering, with some rather questionable description of tribal souls; 'Phenomenology', the realization of self-identity; and 'Psychology', about intuition, memory, etc.; and concludes with 'the unity of the theoretical and the practical spirit as free will'. So now he affects a major transition to moral and social life and its institutions, to the sphere he calls objective spirit.

'Objective spirit' is the most characteristic and I think the most important, though much denigrated, part of his work; it has led to Hegel's being lightly described as the first sociologist. What he says in the *Encyclopaedia* is amplified in the *Philosophy of Right*. He starts with the general concept of law, which is reason objectified in social relations. He thinks that without *some* recognized rules, and even some recognized property, man could not be man. Not that law can really be understood without reference to morality and to state power, to which he now proceeds. But law in some sense is more fundamental than these. Law however could not exist and have meaning for persons who were without a germ of moral sense. And here Hegel makes for the first time a distinction which has influenced all subsequent philosophical discussion, between *Moralität*, the morality of conscience, and *Sittlichkeit* or social ethics. Conscientiousness, individual responsibility, is quite indispensable, is in a sense the kernel of morality; but such maxims as the Kantian 'Act only as you would require everyone else to act in the same circumstances' are without sufficient content, not a sufficient guide to action. (We saw that Kant himself moved on to the idea of a community of free wills.) But more, individual conscience is not infallible, and exclusive emphasis upon it is liable to lead to intolerant fanaticisms.

Moralität is first and foremost 'having good intentions'; but what is a good intention? It is one directed to the welfare of myself and others in appropriate measure; but what is welfare? Not just an algebraic sum of pleasures, as many critics of Bentham have shown. We find we cannot give a content to the concept of welfare without an analysis of human needs and social requirements. This is the sphere of social ethics. Its threefold substance, Hegel says, is to be found in the family, civil society and the state. There is a system of wants or needs ('*Bedürfnisse*') felt to be justified in any given society, only *some* of which, like food and sleep, can be viewed as wants of every individual human being everywhere; some wants vary from place to place, but they are not therefore dispensable. His grouping of these under the headings 'family', 'civil society' and 'state', needs some explanation. In one sense, 'family' means any organization of sex-relations which provides for the bringing up of children; 'civil society' means any organization based on individual agreement for the satisfaction of needs; 'state' means any organization of power for the maintenance of a social order. All forms must involve a minimal degree of rationality, but Hegel describes what he regards as the most rational forms of meeting the requirements for which they exist.

He thinks the ties of kinship and of free agreement are both needed, and should complement one another. Civil society includes all forms of free self-help and mutual help, including the formation of trade-guilds, but also the provision of useful public works, e.g. street lighting and hospitals (in German the sphere of *Polizei*); also, interestingly, the sphere of civil law, or torts and contracts, in which he thinks it vital that the layman as well as the professional lawyer should take part. 'Civil society', he says, 'should be a sort of universal family.' The forming of corporate bodies is a necessary education for citizenship. Hegel is often (but wrongly) supposed to have assigned all powers and functions to the state; it is worth while to note how much in fact he assigns to the sphere of free agreement. These institutions have a life of their own, and should go on in large measure even in the absence of any state enforcement.* Nevertheless, for a satisfactory human society the state as a rational power-organization is also necessary.

He has been much criticized for some of the language he uses about the state. He does say: 'The state is the divine will – spirit present on earth.' But equally he says: 'The state is no work of art; it stands in the world, and so in the sphere of caprice, con-

---

* 'Quakers and Anabaptists are members only of civil society ... Their refusal to defend the state may perhaps be admitted, provided they perform other services instead.'

tingency and error.' Everywhere there is contrast between actuality and ideal; however, idealized concepts of some sort are essential for study of society.* He thinks, surely rightly, that some rational organization of social power is essential for the development of human freedom, which consists not just in not being physically fettered, but in having opportunities of self-development. He thinks this only occurs where the state both recognizes and welcomes the extraneous factors of family and civil society; but also includes the internal factors of legislature, skilled civil service, and a monarch as source of ultimate personal decision. In describing the forms and interactions of these he may indeed be idealizing the Prussian constitution of his time; but maintaining that for any satisfactory state there must be some factors of this kind, he is saying something of general import, even if in the modern state the factor of ultimate personal decision resides rather in president or prime minister than in a hereditary monarch. Into the detail of his political analyses and recommendations we cannot follow him; but he was passionately interested in the politics of his time and in this and his other political works he has much of interest to say. He might be described as by temperament a radical with élitist instincts.

The State, the Spirit of a People, and the World-spirit (Volksgeister und Weltgeist)

Unlike Kant, Hegel does not envisage the goal of history as the emergence of single world-state. For him indeed the acknowledgement of international law is as important an element in the true state as its constitutional law. The former arises out of the mutual recognition of states, which ought to persist even in war, 'as a condition in which we have to take seriously the vanity of our temporal goods', and may be a necessary element in the development of the world-spirit to a state in which there is world-wide consciousness of responsible freedom. This is because the world-spirit for him is manifested in folk-spirits (Volksgeister) – a difficult word to translate, for a 'folk', a cultural concept, is only potentially

---

* Cf. Max Weber's doctrine of the need for 'idealtypes', simplifying and exaggerating particular features, as instruments of social and historical analysis.

a state, though it tends to become one – compare the two senses, cultural and political, of our word 'nationality'). A folk has chosen certain institutions and customs in preference to others, has a culture of its own (in one sense of that word); now, it may not be unimportant for mankind which culture shall predominate, which be subordinate. The evils of war have a justification only when they can be seen to give rise to something generally acknowledged to be a higher civilization; he claims that this has occurred and can occur, and is the element that one can call 'rational' in history. He is quite aware of, and claims to refute, the charge of advocating an *a priori* dogmatic sort of historiography. He thinks that something we are inclined to call 'progress' can be found in the transitions from Oriental, to Greco–Roman, and finally to the European type of state, because this is a continuous progress towards giving every individual inhabitant freedom under a constitution. Such a notion is unknown to Oriental despotism, restricted in the Greco–Roman empire through the institution of slavery. (He is much maligned for terming the third type of state the '*Germanischer Staat*', which of course does not mean 'German' but the new type of state which seems to us to have originated with Charlemagne.)

For him the world-spirit advances through the predominance of better types of state over worse, and he is optimistic enough to believe that this does on the whole occur. He would probably say that a world-state could be no more than a mere superficial mechanism, not standing for any shared ideology as basis of its law, without which there cannot really be a state. (There is certainly nothing of the sort in the United Nations; in the European Community there is a germ of Europeanism which was essential to its foundation, but it is a very frail and tender plant.) He is well aware of the strange accidents and contingencies of history, among which the most important for him is the unforeseeable emergence and often premature death or, again, abnormally long life, of certain 'world-historical individuals', such as Alexander or Lenin or Mao, who unconsciously accomplish something quite different from what they expected, through what Hegel optimistically calls 'the cunning of reason' (*List der Vernunft*). He seems to most of us far too optimistic about the course of history; but is it really just 'a tale told by an idiot, signifying nothing'? It would be hard to write history, any more than to do natural science, upon that assumption; yet we do write history and seek significance in it – we even plunge into making it.

The final phase of spirit is manifest in art, religion and philosophy. I think Hegel's doctrine is that this cannot come about without the world-spirit having reached a certain stage of maturity – at least he says this is true of philosophy. He says for example 'in the state freedom of thought and science has its origin'. There is a certain complementarity in the manifestation of spirit in nature, in history and in the world of thought. Nevertheless, the self-consciousness of absolute spirit is realized only in individuals, 'when the individual is no longer enclosed in his private thoughts, but is become a moment in the life of the infinite'. 'The state is not self thinking thought' – nor indeed are the folk-spirits. There is some parallelism, but not a close parallelism, between the development of outward civilization and of high culture, of art, religion and philosophy.

Art in Hegel's view is linked in its origins with, and in its highest phases demands the transition to, religion. Equally, religion tends towards, leads on to, philosophy. But these transitions do not occur at any given time; art may function for long periods without any contact with religion. It would take us beyond our present scope to follow Hegel's philosophy of art in detail through the three volumes of his *Lectures on Art*, which contain much of interest. Art for him is a discovery of ideal forms in concrete material, and in works which have an individuality of their own. The beauty of nature is indeed a manifestation of spirit, but it is surpassed by the human imagination in a successful work of art. The main types of art he terms symbolical, classical, and romantic. Symbolic art is hieratic, a means of expression of what is religious or magical; classical art is the purest expression of form, but static; romantic art 'delivers itself to the inward life', seeks to show the tension between spirit and its body. Romantic art is for him more or less equated with Christian art. Since romantic art aims to express tension and change, its highest expressions are found in music and poetry, as sculpture and painting are the highest expressions of classical art.

Unlike art, 'religion thinks'. Hegel distinguishes primitive religions (*Naturreligionen*); Greek, Roman and Jewish religions; and finally Christianity as revealed religion. For he considers that Christianity alone, through its doctrine of the Trinity, reveals the universal ('the Father') permeating the particular as 'Holy Spirit', through the person of an individual, 'the Christ'. It is not unfair to conclude that Hegel recommends Christianity as an imaginative or intuitive rendering of his own philosophy. Or, as someone has said, he regards Christianity as exoteric or popular philosophy, and philosophy as an esoteric form of religion.

The account of philosophy as the final phase of 'spirit become self-conscious' is remarkably brief in the *Enclyclopaedia*. It can, I believe, only be understood, when one bears in mind that for Hegel philosophy means both the individual going round the whole circle through which the individual mind progresses towards fuller understanding and also the totality of the stages through which mankind has progressed towards systematic understanding – the history of philosophy. One can only conclude by quoting some of the phrases in which he here characterizes philosophy: it is 'an elevation of man's spirit through purification of his knowledge from all merely subjective opinions, and the purification of his will from all selfishness of desires'. 'Its ultimate aim is to reconcile thought (or conception) with reality' – words from the conclusion of the *History of Philosophy*. The task of envisaging the world as it really is is for him a religious task; but by no means, as Bradley and others have represented it, a sinking of the individual in mystical feeling of the absolute. It is a task rather of thinking and re-thinking and again re-thinking one's experience, observational, moral and cultural, until we may say that in a certain sense reality becomes conscious in us. Since it includes the search for truthfulness in the activities of family, social life and citizenship, it represents a not ignoble way of life.

For a clear idea of how Hegel's mind worked read the *Philosophy of Right*, the *Philosophy of Mind*, then the first three sections of the *Phenomenology*. To read Hegel completely 'without tears' is a forlorn hope.

5

The Aftermath of German Idealism: (1) Schopenhauer and Nietzsche

There are evidently connections between great political changes and changes in that radical mode of thought which we call philosophy, but we must not expect any very close parallelism. Yet the final defeat of the French Revolution by Napoleon's abdication in 1815, and the publication of Hegel's system, both appear to us to mark the end of an epoch. Those who view this sytem as the last of the constructive metaphysical efforts of the European mind hold that after this, philosophy is superseded by science. Schelling indeed lived on until 1854, but his later work is much less characteristic of German idealism, and represents the spirit of a new, disillusioned, more positivistic age. Later Romanticism can be seen as sober, disillusioned, by contrast with its earlier, heroic tones. This is true of the art of the period, as well as of the philosophy of Schopenhauer and the 'Left-Hegelians', whom we have now to consider.

Arthur Schopenhauer (1788–1860) can be viewed as a child of German Idealism. Indeed, in the sense in which 'idealism' is generally used in England, as equivalent to Berkeleyan idealism – *esse est percipi* – Schopenhauer is far more of an idealist than any of the rest, for he holds (if with some inconsistencies) that what we call real things consist only of ideas or representations in human consciousness. He maintains at the close of his principal work, *The World as Will and Idea*, that if the human race would only practise complete sexual abstinence, not merely would the human race die out but 'the weaker reflection of it would also pass away, as the twilight vanishes along with the full light. With the entire abolition of knowledge the rest of the world would vanish into nothing, for without a subject there would be no object.' Yet he claimed that he was the one and only true disciple of Kant, and poured abuse upon Fichte, Schelling and Hegel, whom he called 'the three celebrated sophists' – Hegel being 'that intellectual Caliban'.

Schopenhauer's philosophy must be seen as the expression of his temperament to a great extent and of the milieu in which he lived, which differed greatly from that of the 'celebrated sophists'. His father was a well-to-do Danzig banker, and Arthur, after one unsuccessful attempt to lecture in Berlin, led a comfortable life with a good deal of travel. He wrote in a lively, leisurely style, his thoughts reinforced with many striking illustrations. His great work, *The World as Will and Idea*, though published in 1818, did not become really popular until the publication of his book of essays, *Parerga und Paralipomena* in 1851.

It seems undeniable that Schopenhauer was a vain, suspicious and quarrelsome man, and that he enjoyed the so-called good things of life in a way hardly in accord with the saintly asceticism recommended in his works. Yet his philosophy should not for that reason be ignored. Not merely was its influence great – upon Nietzsche and, *via* von Hartmann, upon Freud – it is important because it states in European terms familiar to us one of the major alternative visions of the world which has a perennial attraction for many, not only in its Asian homeland but also for us Europeans. It is a type of philosophy which demands to be faced and thought through. Its keynotes are: denial of the individual will, suppression of desires, total sympathy with all life, assertion and realization of each man's literal identity with every other, the opting out of the struggle of life through detached contemplation and asceticism. This type of philosophy had a special appeal in the disillusionment of the first half of the nineteenth century, but it represents a perennial possibility.

Schopenhauer's work can most simply be viewed as the attempt to transplant to Europe the philosophy of the *Upanishads* and of Theravadin Buddhism, and to present this as the natural consequence of a true interpretation of the philosophy of Kant. For him the central point of Kant's philosophy is his distinction between phenomena or appearances and the thing-in-itself. Kant indeed, as we saw, always talks about things-in-themselves, in the plural, and recognizes other sorts of *noumena* or thinkables as well. Schopenhauer however regards all this as a sign of weakness, of concession to common-sense thought by Kant; he maintains that it is impossible to hold together the two sides – epistemological and practical – of Kant's philosophy except by recognizing that there is but one thing-in-itself, the will, of which all else is appearance or phenomenon – as Schopenhauer calls it, representation or idea (*Vorstellung*). It is however not just my idea or yours, but an idea of the cosmic will. (Unlike Berkeley's ideas, which were only in the mind of God when they were not in anyone else's mind, everything that is is an appearance of the cosmic will.)

We think there are separate individuals with separate streams of consciousness, but this is illusion. The illusion is due to the forms of space and time and the categories of substantiality and causality, which, according to Kant, we inevitably impose upon our experience. Kant explicitly refused to allow that this made it illusory. For Schopenhauer however these forms are equivalent to the classical Indian concept of the veil of Maya, which conceals from us the unity of all that there is – the Atman-Brahman – making us see multiplicity where there is really unity.

Schopenhauer believed he could simplify Kant by attributing both the experience of space and time and the experience of thinghood to one formal principle, which he called the 'principle of sufficient reason', manifesting itself in geometrical and arithmetical relations, causal relations and motivational relations. Why there should be this principle, driving us to split up the world in the way we do, is for him one of 'the two inexplicables'. About the will and its self-splitting nothing more can be said; it is just the way things are, and the way our understanding works. In to the detail of how this principle of multiplicity works we need not follow him. For him 'individual' means only that which is, or rather appears to be, causally effective – *wirklich*, the German word for 'real', that which works.

Such working we experience in the first instance in ourselves as 'will'; but we see that all causation in nature is analogous to it. (Hume had denied that we have such immediate experience of willing; Schopenhauer allows that we experience it in the feelings of pleasure or unpleasure which invariably accompany willing.) The manifestation of the cosmic will in human beings being its most complete form, we are justified, he maintains, in using the word 'will' to describe all the apparent activity that we detect in nature. But it is important to recognize the various 'grades of objectification' of the will, as he calls them. These grades run from simple physical force, through the dull, plant-like consciousness of animal bodies, up to full human awareness.

For the will objectifies itself in bodies; 'my body is my will become visible', and is the immediate object of my perception. All things are appearances, but some are less merely-apparent than others (to adapt Orwell's famous remark about the pigs). All are ideas, yet the world of ideas is 'the complete mirror of the will', so that we can discern something of a real structure in it, especially, as we shall see, in detached artistic contemplation of it. There are archetypal ideas (similar to those of Plato) which the various types of body in the world are said to mirror. Schopenhauer aimed to construct a pure monism, in which nothing is real but the one will – but such a pure monism without any distinctions must be ineffable.

He is a Romantic, diverging sharply from the spirit of the Enlightenment in making feeling, not reason, the basis of all morality as well as of art. Sensation (*Empfindung*) is a species of feeling (*Gefühl*). Reason gives us no immediate knowledge and is altogether subordinate. I *feel* my will all the time in the movement of my body, for the act of will and the movement of body are one and the same. It is in my body that I first experience the per-petual conflict between its different forms which is the chief feature of the will. This is what leads us to regard it as the 'will-to-live', for it objectifies itself in many different forces and forms, of which the higher endeavours always to conquer the lower. What the words 'higher' and 'lower' mean, we can only understand if we adopt a contemplative attitude towards nature, the attitude characteristic of art. We feel this conflict however as a conflict between different individuals' will-to-live, and we feel this as a chief cause of suffering, for him the most outstanding feature of the world. We must not think of the will as aiming in any way to promote the higher forms at the expense of the lower; the will is blind, and all conflict is due to the fact that it has, inscrutably, split itself up into a multiplicity of individuals, each apparently willing to maintain itself in being.

Suffering is the outstanding feature of the world, and the only escape from it lies in absolute denial of one's individuality, the complete realization of the essence of the *Upanishads*, the '*Tat tvam asi*' – 'that other art thou!' For him, morality can only mean mitigation of suffering. All moral evil consists in acts which thwart the will-to-live of another, so causing additional suffering. Prevention of such additional suffering is for him the only proper sphere of law, of the action of public authority. But such morally-wrong acts are not the only source of suffering; and it might well be thought that since all acts are the product of the cosmic will – the only true reality – the whole notion of morality is out of place. For him morality, in the sense of refraining from injuring others, is something outward and superficial; the true end of life is calm detachment, is 'to attain such a clear picture of our true selves that this picture of ourselves may calm us'. He rejects Kant's and Fichte's postulation of moral freedom in our acts, but allows that the individual can exercise a certain control of his attitudes and sentiments, that he can strive for a calm detachment in face of desire.

Such calm detachment can be achieved for a time through the contemplation – and if one is a genius, through the creation – of art. But it can only finally be achieved through a form of asceticism, which is a complete denial of the will-to-live, of which sexual abstinence is the most important element.

Schopenhauer's aesthetic theories are one of the most interesting and enduring parts of his work. There is surely much truth – though it is not the whole truth – in the 'detachment theory' which demands that we should learn to see things apart from their utility, to recollect in tranquillity. In so far as all art idealizes in some sense, does not simply copy, it gropes after the archetypes embodied in species or grades of being, which Schopenhauer called the 'ideas' (*Ideen*, not *Vorstellungen*). In the gradual purification of art from all utility we can discern, he thinks, a certain order: architecture is less pure than landscape gardening; this less pure than the portrayal of animal and plant life; the highest degree of purity can be achieved in the portrayal of the human form. The highest forms of art for him are to be found, first, in tragedy, which satisfies us through providing for our contemplation a picture of the conflicts of the will with itself, together with a sort or resolution of them; and second, in music, which mirrors the very rhythm of the will, its unity in multiplicity. Art is the product of a genius, who is distinguished from the common mass of mankind by the wealth of his imagination, which overlays and far outstrips his perception, and so helps to subdue his desires.

But production and contemplation of art can afford only a temporary respite from the demands of the will-to-live, which presses upon us at one time with imperative needs, at another with boredom. From this, only absolute self-denial can bring release, and this involves suicide by self-starvation – no other form of suicide can guarantee freedom from the will after death.[1]

It should not be denied that this type of Jainist–Buddhist philosophy has its appeal, especially to those who, as Schopenhauer probably was, are very sensitive to pain and to the suffering of the world. Can it be lived with complete sincerity – for it claims to be a programme for life? In his essay, 'Schopenhauer as Educator' – which incidentally tells us little about Schopenhauer – Nietzsche praises him for his truthfulness and cheerfulness (*'Wahrhaftigkeit und Heiterkeit'*). Cheerfulness is certainly quite compatible with theoretical metaphysical pessimism about the world. But truthfulness in the fullest sense? This surely requires that a man's life accord with his professed beliefs, which was far from being the case with Schopenhauer. Do we in fact find this accord in those who profess life-denying philosophies – those who practise the extremes of asceticism like the Buddha's first companions, or rush to be martyred like the early Christians? This was one of the questions that Nietzsche set himself to answer.

Friedrich Nietzsche (1844–1900) is not only important for his influence upon subsequent European literature – André Gide, André Malraux, Albert Camus, J.-P. Sartre, G.B. Shaw, W.B. Yeats, Rilke, George, Thomas Mann – he is immensely important for an understanding of the age we have lived through and are living through. He gave European philosophy a new twist, which is the origin of much in Existentialism, but also, I think, of much in Freud and in Wittgenstein. His work is immensely difficult to characterize fairly within the compass of such a book as this, difficult both because of his – largely aphoristic – manner of writing, and because of the character of his philosophy, which was not intended for professional writing-tables or learned journals. His *Twilight of the Idols* has the sub-title 'Philosophy with a Hammer', the hammer being, as we learn, not an instrument of destruction but one for testing and showing up the hollowness of popular idols. He wrote with the intention of provoking, or as he called it 'educating', for he regarded the philosopher neither as an entertainer nor as a specialist in curious and remote questions. In his early work, 'Schopenhauer as Educator', he in great part describes his own aims. He certainly had the ability to provoke, to be like Socrates the gadfly of his time, for he had an extraordinary command of language; a well-known opponent of his philosophy once described him to the author as the most splendid German writer since Luther. (That this was a temptation to him we shall have to consider later.) It was a power that he sometimes abused.

His work has called forth extremes of enthusiasm and of hostility and an astonishing number of interpretations. In the First World War British propaganda frequently mentioned him – along with the historian, Treitschke – as one of the intellectual instigators of the war and exponent of 'Prussianism'. In the Second World War it was his fate to be utilized by the German propagandists; Hitler's last present to Mussolini was a sumptuous edition of Nietzsche's complete works. It can now be definitely asserted that no serious scholar regards him either as having supported the nationalism of the Bismarckian Empire or, still less, as having favoured anti-Semitism or a doctrine of racial purity.* Nothing in his work is clearer than his dislike of the new German nationalism – 'we Europeans', 'good Europeans', are favourite expressions with him – or, apart from a few witticisms, his immense respect for the Jews and Judaism and their vital contribution to European culture.

Nevertheless, ignoring these obvious misinterpretations of servile propagandists, there is still room left for much difference of interpretation. This is certainly not due to obscurity, as in the case of Hegel. Nor, I think, is it due to inconsistency, unless to the inconsistency which can be found between his finished work and the uncoordinated notes published by his sister during his last illness – on the whole these must just be discounted. A more serious problem is presented by his aphoristic manner of writing. His *Thus Spoke Zarathustra* – a very great work – is philosophy in an imaginative, poetical guise; he called it 'an experiment in dithyrambic writing'. It has a certain kinship with the poems of Pindar and of the old pre-Socratic philosophers of Greece; how successful the experiment was we shall have to consider.†

Again, a large part of his work consists in aphorisms, a medium seemingly derived from La Rochefoucauld and Pascal, both of whom he admired. This means that he gives us views on the same subject again and again in different places, and often in a context which is occasional and polemical. A writer with his powers is often in danger of sacrificing truth for effect. Whether he confuses the differing aims of poetry and philosophy is another question.

Owing to his aphoristic style, inconsistencies of statement can

* The complication deriving from the fact that his anti-Semitic sister took possession of his notes, published what she thought fit, and was not above forgery, has now been sufficiently exposed by scholars.

† The Levy series of translations, long the only obtainable translations in English, make it appear a parody of the Bible, which was certainly not Nietzsche's intention. Nor is this style at all true to the character of the original. He frequently stressed that he was not trying to found a new religion or quasi-religion. Irony is perhaps the most striking feature of his style, and there is singularly little irony, if any, to be found in the Bible. There is a close kinship of his style with that of Heine, whom he much admired.

easily be found; did he perhaps merely want to put down his observations on life as they occurred to him? I think this is clearly not the case. In the first place, his post-*Zarathustra* works, *Beyond Good and Evil* and *The Genealogy of Morals*, which were intended as parts of a major treatise on the will-to-power, are written in an almost continuous prose. More important, he had a forcible and clear conception of the vocation of the philosopher, who is to give a comprehensive and consistent view of life – even if the philosopher's peculiar will-to-power knowingly makes the world rather more consistent than it really is,[2] and even if he must always aim to enliven, not just instruct.* Nietzsche must therefore stand criticism as a philosopher, not merely as a poet; indeed, the desire to get at the truth seems a passion with him as with Socrates – a passion not overlaid as so often with others, by disputes with colleagues or desire for a nicely-rounded system. This is not to say however that he was equally interested in all the traditional subject-matter of philosophy. He has a good deal to say, but mostly in the notes for the 'Will to Power' (a suspect source), about natural science; about Schopenhauer's type of mystical philosophy; he is in general terms a realist, assuming that reality is by no means the creation of our senses, however great may be the element of conjecture, and even of fashion (*Zurechtlegung*), in our view of what is real. Above all things for him stands the unity of the human person; the human body is the most complete expression, or 'diagram', of the varieties and tensions we experience in consciousness, of rationality and irrationality. He has the metaphysician's urge to make the whole world thinkable which leads him tentatively to extend the concept of the will-to-power to the sources of energy in non-human nature, as a useful concept to explain what is and what happens.[3] But it is as a philosopher of culture and as a depth-psychologist that he is outstanding; his philosophy of man in his environment is wide-ranging, goes deep, and, as I believe, is consistent – reasonable allowance being made for the development which takes place as the ideas of any major writer unfold.

---

* Nietzsche prefaces his *Untimely Reflections* (*Unzeitgemässe Betrachtungen*) with this Goethe quotation: 'I detest anything that just instructs me without increasing my activity or enlightening me directly.'

Friedrich Nietzsche was born in Rocken in what is now East Germany in 1844, son of a Lutheran pastor who died within five years of his birth. He attended the famous boarding-school of Schul-Pforta in Saxony, at which Fichte and many distinguished men had been pupils. There he acquired his enthusiasm for the study of Greek and Roman civilizations, which he continued at Leipzig and Bonn Universities, discovering Schopenhauer in a second-hand shop in 1865. In 1868 he met Richard Wagner, who was to be the second great influence upon his life – apart from the Greeks. In 1870, at the extraordinarily early age of twenty-six, he was made full Professor of Classical Philology at the University of Basel. However the Franco–Prussian War had just broken out, and he volunteered at once as a medical orderly, with the result that he returned to Basel that year, with his health shattered by severe dysentery and diphtheria contracted during his army service. He suffered from migraine and general ill-health for the next ten years, and in 1879 felt obliged to resign from the university. He lived much in Italy and in the high Alps, on a small pension, for the succeeding ten years. His works are full of images drawn from the life of the Italian Mediterranean and the Engadine, both of which he loved passionately; much of *Zarathustra* was composed on long walks in the mountains.

Apart from Richard Wagner, the most important influence on Nietzsche's life was his deep friendship and later breach in 1876 with the extremely intelligent Lou Salomé, later Rilke's mistress. He lived a retired life on a small pension, and his health – especially his eyesight – continuously worsened. By 1888 his work, long totally ignored, began to be known and the Dane, Georg Brandes, gave public lectures on him at Copenhagen University. But also the first signs of his final illness had begun to show themselves that same year. The next year he collapsed unconscious in the streets of Turin and was taken to Basel, where he was declared insane on the basis of some odd letters to Overbeck, one signed 'Dionysus'. About this illness, which of course delighted his Christian opponents, there has been much dispute; it seems on the whole to have been a form of paralysis, possibly syphilitic, though he certainly suffered from some delusions, especially identifying himself with the Greek god Dionysus. At any rate he lived completely *incommunicado* with his sister, without writing anything more, until his death in 1900.

The facts of his life are certainly relevant to his work; but how? His last works, *Ecce Homo* and *Antichrist*, certainly betray an increased violence of expression which may be attributed to the onset of the disease, but few will now agree with his enemies in discounting most of his work as the product of a madman, or see their view confirmed by the marvellous account of the nature of inspiration which we find in *Ecce Homo* (sections 3 and 4): 'a state of great health, my whole body enthusiastic, let alone my soul. I used to walk seven or eight hours over the mountains, sleeping well, full of vigour and patience.' In this euphoric state he composed the first three parts of *Zarathustra*, each part in around ten days; the last part is later, written in Nice and Menton.

One may regard his pre-*Zarathustra* works as tentative thought-experiments on the novel problems which at that time seemed vital to him. Then as he became clearer about these he composed *Zarathustra* as a sort of imaginative preview of what was to be later worked out in sober prose. I shall attempt first to say something about the principal motifs of the earlier works; then about the form and content of *Zarathustra*; finally, with reference to his later works, about the main concepts of his system of thought – of the 'transvaluation of values', the 'superman', 'eternal recurrence', the relation between life and reason, and the assault on Christianity which this entailed.

His early works, full of good observations (the latter part of *Gay Science* – *Fröhliche Wissenschaft* – was written after *Zarathustra*), are interesting as throwing light on his development. He starts from an immersion in Greek thought, both of the classical and post-classical age, a phil-Hellenism far more concerned with the ideas and ideals of Greece than with the detail of its language – which used to loom so large in the English system of education! But influenced perhaps by his friend the great scholar Rohde's work on the soul, his first work, *The Birth of Tragedy from the Spirit of Music*, emphasizes the one-sidedness of the prevailing –

what he called the 'Apollonian' – view of classical humanism, that in Greek art all is light, clarity, self-restraint. Against this he pointed to the wild and passionate elements in the Greek view of nature and human nature, which he was to term the 'Dionysian' (from Dionysus, god of wine, whose worship was central to certain orgiastic 'mysteries' in the country, in which the Greeks let themselves go from time to time, and also – be it noted – to the creation of tragedy itself, which grew out of the Dionysus-festival dances). In this early essay he holds that the Dionysian element was rationalized out of tragedy under the influence of Socrates, making it less revealing than it might be. At this early stage of his thought he merely demands that 'Dionysus' must have his proper place in life, and regards Apollo and Dionysus merely as symbolizing different, essentially antagonistic poles in life. But much of his later work is a sustained attempt to see them as a unity in a life which he will call 'Dionysian' in a new sense, one which accepts and masters the Dionysian factors of passion and suffering.

This work is followed by the short but extremely influential essay entitled 'On the Uses and Dangers of History for Life'. Perhaps influenced by his friend at Basel, the great historian, Burckhardt, he maintains that the study of history, especially of classical history, has become just a vehicle of instruction, no longer something that can enliven (Goethe) and inspire. He distinguishes three legitimate uses of history – to set up inspiring goals; to give us a love for the obscure detail of our everyday past; to help us to see what is going wrong in the present. Above all he warns against our being suffocated with history, obsessed with the idea that everything worth while has already been done, or that all values are transitory. We need to search in history for the manifestation of values that are super-historical, those of the great artist, the great philosopher, the great saint; these values are in a sense timeless; there is no necessary progress in history.

In his next work, *Human, All Too Human*, he takes up for the first time the subject of the psychological effects of religion, and of Christianity in particular. Christianity has been largely concerned to instil in men a sense of guilt, which is often not founded in any objective acts. It tries to inculcate a general sense of guilt for merely being alive (original sin); this results in cruelty both towards others and towards oneself. Further, it tends to devalue all that is healthy, capable, excellent in this life, for the sake of salvation in another life, cultivating a sort of humility which conceals a neurotic will-to-power. Finally, it preaches a God whose essential nature is to punish, but who also grants indiscriminate salvation to those who believe, thus undermining men's respect for the very kernel of morality. Quoting from the Catholic poet, Novalis, who, he says, ought to know, he finds it 'wonderful that men have not long ago recognized the intimate association that exists between lust, religion and cruelty'. Much of this has become a commonplace in our time, mainly through Freud; it was by no means the case in Nietzsche's day – rather, this was the first time, so far as I know, that anything of the sort could appear in print. (It is of course developed in more detail in his later work, especially in *Antichrist*.)

Untimely Reflections contains the first version of his criticism of the modern state, of its current equation of political power in the international field with success.

His next work, *Dawn*, continues his psychological criticism of Christianity, especially of its cult of indiscriminate pity, which really implies a lack of respect for human dignity, the treatment of people as objects, incapable of any responsibility for their own fate. It is at the end of this work that we first have the image of the madman, running through the streets of the town crying 'God is Dead!' But so far he does not go beyond displaying the contrast between the 'healthy virtues' of the Greeks, their valuation of courage, justice, self-control, wisdom and generosity, and the Christian cultivation of an unhealthy sense of sinfulness, with its corollaries of a demand for unlimited self-sacrifice and a magical salvation. He was deeply impressed with these features of the Christian culture of his time; he felt Schopenhauer's radical life-denial to be no solution. For the development of his own constructive ideas – if such they were – for the regeneration of culture, we must await *Zarathustra* and the later works.

To give some account of the great, if uneven, philosophical poem, *Thus Spoke Zarathustra*, is immensely difficult. But it is a great poem, and anyone concerned with the kind of questions

Nietzsche had at heart should surely attempt to read it. At the present time questions about the revaluation of values and the destiny of our European culture can hardly be avoided, except by those who deliberately pass by on the other side. Nietzsche felt himself, and rightly, to be living in an era of cultural crisis, in which new values connected with industrialization, nationalism and mass-democracy troubled men's minds, along with a feeling of religious emptiness. Until recently the poem was almost inaccessible to English readers, so bad were the available translations, but good translations are now available, which give a fair rendering of the spirit, if not of the music of the original. It must be conceded that much of it is ear-untranslatable, such are Nietzsche's tricks – bad ones, on the whole – with the German language, utilizing puns, assonance, double and contrasting meanings, etymological versus current meanings; yet he is capable of entrancing the ear by passages of direct, simple poetry. *Zarathustra* is certainly too long, and would benefit from cutting. Nietzsche too often could not resist a chance of getting in a witty dig at some opponent. This leads to a change in the character of the poem in the course of the first three parts; one feels it is less Zarathustra and more Nietzsche who is speaking. The mythical character emerges again however in part four, which was written much later in Nice and Menton.

What led him to adopt this unusual form for the exposition of his ideas? Mainly, I believe, the wish to startle the educated public of his time, people who would not read a philosophical treatise; also to introduce two new conceptions, those of 'superman' and of 'eternal recurrence', which he did not as yet feel able to develop in sober prose.*

Most of part one of *Zarathustra* is magnificent straightforward German, and can be enjoyed without explanation of any esoteric symbolisms. The encounter of Zarathustra with the old hermit who

---

* With great respect to Walter Kaufmann, I have preferred to retain the translation 'superman' for *Übermensch*, on the ground (1) that it has already come into our language through Bernard Shaw and other distinguished writers; (2) that 'superhuman' and 'subhuman' are meaningful English words, whereas 'overman' suggests nothing. 'English' and 'American' have gone different ways over this usage of 'superman', etc.

does not know that God is dead and with the tightrope-walker; the parable of the camel, the lion and the child are simple enough, and live in the memory as pictures. The parable pictures the three stages which Nietzsche thought were needed for a revival of culture: the stages of disciplined acceptance, of revolt, and of creative living-out what you have found to be good, no longer as a burden but as a delight (the child). For the rest, most of part one is fairly obviously directed against what he felt as the decadence of his age: the egregious 'last men', seekers of a sequence of little pleasures for the day and for the night; the 'teachers of virtue' who are no more than teachers of how to achieve untroubled sleep; the 'unwordly' who depreciate this world for the sake of an after-world; the 'despisers of the body' who go in fear of their passions, especially of sex; reading and writing – the fantastic over-valuation of mere literacy; 'the pale victim' of the law whose justice is really revenge; 'the new idol' of the mass-state; 'free death' (deciding to die at the right time); 'the thousand and one goals'. This last is I think important for his later theory of the origination and transvaluation of values.

This argument is taken up again in part two, in the section 'On Self-overcoming', important for the conceptions of will-to-power and 'superman'; and again in part three, in 'The Old and the New Tablets'. In part two, the sections 'On Priests', 'On Scholars' and 'On Poets' are fundamental; the sections 'On the Tarantulas' and 'On Great Events' give his forceful views on mass-democracy and the socialism of his day.

Part three is mainly concerned with his new thought – of the 'eternal recurrence of the same' – and his reluctance to accept it (he believed, but erroneously, that it could be mathematically proved that it must be so). Songs are now introduced for the first time. Of these, some like the 'First Dancing Song', on the tensions between life and wisdom, and the 'Yea-and-Amen Song', are of great importance for an understanding of the whole; others seem just exercises in all-too-Wagnerian poetry, which one may or may not care for. In part four we have the deliberate parody of Wagner, in the rather tiresome 'Song of the Daughters of the Wilderness', with its somewhat heavy-handed humour.

Part four in a way reverts to the beginning; it contains comparatively little discourse, and is in the main an imaginative myth. Dramatically, it is supposed to have occurred many years later than the previous events in Zarathustra's life. In it Nietzsche pictures the companions of his own youth, who at one time or other of his life he had seen as his teachers, as 'bridges to superman'. It is full of symbolism, some obvious like 'the high noon', some which I do not claim to understand fully. The guests who now come to Zarathustra, and whom he addresses as 'the higher men' are: Schopenhauer (old sooth-sayer); the Kings (representing the simple-minded, old-fashioned aristocracy); the blood-sucking leech (the ideal scientist, perhaps Rohde); Wagner (the old conjurer); the last Pope; the ugliest man (he of greatest misfortune); Jesus (the voluntary beggar); finally Zarathustra's shadow (his special tempter – to self-pity). As can be seen, some are mythical personages, and others are real persons mythified as incorporating a certain idea or attitude to life. They are all 'men of great longing' and out of tune with their times. Their chief failing, in Nietzsche's eyes, is that they cannot laugh at themselves, are weighed down by their new insights, cannot realize how much is still possible! The treatment of the old Pope, who has ceased to believe, but whose natural piety means that all his life he has been accustomed to bless, illustrates Nietzsche's remark about himself as *'Frommster aller Gottlosen'* – 'most pious of the godless'.

Much wisdom is concentrated in his discourse, 'The Higher Men', at the Supper, a conscious parody of the Christian rite. (It is followed by the 'Adoration of the Ass', a tiresome and unworthy section, in my judgement.) 'Little perfect things you should keep around you; how rich is the earth in little perfect things! . . . Do not be virtuous beyond your strength; there is a wicked falsity in those who do . . . You higher men, have you not all failed? Be of good cheer, how much is still possible! Learn to laugh at yourselves, as one must laugh!'[3]

But this is just what they cannot do. As morning breaks they form up into a solemn procession to go to greet Zarathustra; his lion gives a great roar and they flee in terror. "'My pity for the higher men," thinks Zarathustra, "what does it matter? Am I concerned for happiness? I am concerned for my work." And he left his cave, glowing and strong like the morning sun that shines out of dark mountains.'

Perhaps philosophical myth is not to every man's taste; it is a genre not much attempted since Plato. Much of *Zarathustra* can be skipped or skimmed; but much must be read attentively to grasp Nietzsche's main philosophical conceptions: will-to-power, superman, eternal recurrence and the transvaluation of all values. We must now address ourselves to his important prose works, subsequent to *Zarathustra*, in which these are developed: *Beyond Good and Evil*, *The Genealogy of Morals*, *Antichrist*, the notes on nihilism, and the autobiographical *Ecce Homo*. (I find the *Twilight of the Idols* less important, and omit the polemical works against Wagner as somewhat beyond the scope of this book. We have already had a taste in *Zarathustra* of his feeling against the irresponsible falsity of the romantic poet.) We know Nietzsche had it in mind to write a more metaphysical 'Will-to-Power', but changed its title to *Umwertung aller Werte* or *Transvaluation of All Values*. There is no doubt that he regarded this as the task *par excellence* of the philosopher, although his observations of nature are by no means without interest. The philosopher must try to understand how values emerge and change, how they are related to one another and to natural and social fact and to supposed fact. To this task the concepts of superman and of eternal recurrence are subordinate; and his criticism of Christianity is of the essence. To begin with, he had to break down the idea that there is just morality and immorality (or, as is said today, just morality and permissiveness). Schopenhauer indeed had breached this idea with his doctrine that a rigorously life-denying morality is a perfectly possible one; but we find no trace of it in any previous German philosopher. (The idea of a pagan and a Christian morality was perhaps beginning to emerge in England about the same time in such writers as Matthew Arnold and Lecky.) In our century the idea is now perhaps fairly familiar, through the work of anthropologists and sociologists.[4]

There is no doubt a sense in which the 'moral' can mean a type of action or attitude that is *sui generis* – with its contrast the 'immoral' and the 'amoral': the faithful burning of heretics was no doubt a moral duty within the current morality of the Church of the fifteenth century. Nietzsche is well aware of this, and so writes not of moralities but of systems or 'tables' of values. So far as I know, he was the first to put forward a theory – crude perhaps, in view of the researches carried out since his time – of the origination and establishment of systems of value or moralities.

The theory developed in *Beyond Good and Evil* and its sequel is that a system of values is always developed by an aristocracy (*die Vornehmen*) and that 'good' originally signifies the qualities required in the members of the aristocracy to keep them in power in the kind of life they have chosen. An example: the change in the sense of *agathos* and *areté* from the times of the Homeric aristocracy to those of the classical Greek city-dwelling aristocracy has been exactly traced. In the so-called underdeveloped countries in our own day we are surrounded by cultural change of this sort, about which much has been written.[5] Nietzsche is of course far from thinking that just any system of values can be created by individuals who are powerful enough; they are necessarily related to the needs of a certain society in a certain environment – as he told us, imaginatively, in 'The Thousand and One Goals'. In such an aristocratic morality the antitheses are between 'good' and 'bad' (*gut* and *schlecht*), 'bad' for the approved life of the group – as e.g. cowardly or treacherous conduct. The notion of 'evil' or 'wicked' (*böse*) has no place in their morality – it has often been observed that there is no real equivalent word for this in classical Greek. The aristocratic man can indeed be impious, offend against the gods of the tribe, often unknowingly, as Oedipus did; but such conduct is not valued as immoral or wicked – a conception, according to Nietzsche, which arises only in subject-classes, or, in the Judeo-Christian case, through a special kind of priestly aristocracy concerned to maintain a special kind of life and to impose its will on a subject-class.

In all systems of values Nietzsche recognizes that there is some criterion which leads us to single out certain acts and attitudes as moral, and not just sensible or agreeable. This is the free acceptance of responsibility which he calls the ability to keep promises. Have I *undertaken* to fight along with you, to accept you as my guest – it is this that makes the difference. This is why a child cannot act morally or immorally: until (as Piaget thinks) about the age of ten, he cannot understand the meaning of a promise and be thought able to carry it out.

Now the subject-class does not as such create systems of values to maintain itself in power (though of course, as we now see much more clearly, there are always arising within its groups rival élites, who put forth values intended to compete with those of the dominant élite or élites). The typical member of the subject-class understands 'good' in the sense of what has been laid down for him by some alien will, and what is disapproved he looks upon with horror as evil or wicked. To these different conceptions of wrong correspond the different conceptions of virtue; to the aristocratic class these are courage, loyalty, generosity, piety towards the country's gods regarded as a sort of superior, if rather incalculable, kin. For the subject-class on the other hand 'good' means above all abstention from what is forbidden by the rules or commandments. (But too much stress must not be laid on whether these attitudes are formulated negatively or positively; there can be, as with the young man in the gospel, a delight in 'having kept all these things from my youth', while 'not slandering one's neighbour' (Psalm xv) may be a sign of a deep attachment to truth.) Positive virtues of the subject-class, which does not aspire to be anything else, will be unlimited compassion for 'the poor' as such, the assumption that these are 'the good', the urge to relieve any suffering at any cost of creative effort and the demand that everyone should be kept just alive somehow. These are the virtues of the 'last men' of *Zarathustra* part one.

But the whole situation is complicated where there is a priestly aristocracy – for example, among Hindus, Jews and Christians. For like others, it promotes a system of values which upholds its will-to-power in its preferred style of life, which is not that of a military, agricultural, or mercantile aristocracy. As with these others, it gives rise to outstanding individuals, such as Moses or Jesus, who set their individual seal upon this system of values out of which they emerged, and without which they could not have emerged.

A priestly aristocracy is one with an ascetic ideal of life. Now asceticism – the original Greek *askesis* just means training, e.g. for a race – is a word with a wide spread of meaning. Some *askesis* is necessary for every healthy person, is at the heart of that *Selbst-überwindung* ('self-overcoming') which Nietzsche said was an essential of superman. But asceticism can go far beyond anything of this sort, and become a form of self-torture, a contempt for the ordinary good things of life, whereas Nietzsche says that one of the features of aristocracy is a great thankfulness. There is again a certain special asceticism of scholars and philosophers – how many of the latter, he asks, have been happily married? But that of the ascetic priest is a special kind, directed towards finding a rationale for his sufferings, due to his sense of his sins. It is this which has led to the enormously important part he has played in our traditional value-system as developed by Paul. Paul managed to bring into currency a code of values which instilled into the depths of men's minds the idea that all their sufferings were due to their sin. (But this doctrine took on better with the subject-classes than with the ruling classes – who had their own standard – and led to the equation of the 'mighty' with the 'wicked'.) Such heightened feelings of guilt led men to see life as a vale of misery rather than to rejoice in it. And for those not capable of rigorous ascetic practices to allay these feelings, the priest offered a simple remedy: the profession of belief in formulae laid down for salvation through the death of the Saviour; abstention from what has been labelled as sinful by the code; relief for their self-pity as suffering sinners by cultivation of indiscriminate pity for others. Nietzsche writes[6] that the sheep says, 'I suffer, someone must be to blame.' But the shepherd, the ascetic priest, says to him, 'Quite so, somebody must be to blame, but you are that somebody, you alone are to blame.' This sort of religion has persisted so long because it has served a useful purpose in keeping the subject-classes quiet; it has supplied what Marx was to call 'opium for the people'. Not all priestly aristocracies have developed in just this way, however, as Nietzsche shows by a comparison of the Jewish rabbinate, the Brahmin and Buddhist 'priesthoods'.

Religion as such, he says, is akin to serious art in its value and in its dangers. Both derive from a desire to celebrate the beauty and secret wisdom of the world, in spite of the immense element of chance and of suffering which it also contains. Both are liable to involve man in a radical disregard for truth – 'the poets tell too many lies.' Judaism, on the whole a more honourable religion than Christianity, naturally has certain features in common with its offshoot – overvaluation of the poor and of mere abstention from sin; but it has blessed and made significant the ordinary events of life.

Jesus, so far as we can discover, set himself in great part to dispel the sense of having offended a jealous God; this was for him the 'good news'. But in Nietzsche's opinion, 'there has been only one Christian and he died on the cross.' In the youthful, apocalyptic enthusiasm which was so characteristic of his age, he preached the giving up of all wordly activities; 'he died too young!' And so he left the way open to Paul to base upon his personal visions the new religion of universal salvation through faith in Christ – at the cost of a knowing deception.

Christianity, says Nietzsche, gave the individual a sense of absolute value; it proved a means of self-maintenance. And when we think of the good social inventions which it has called forth, we cannot deny that it has been a positive factor in our culture. Nevertheless, the negative items in the balance sheet are very heavy – its cultivation of envy of all that is outstanding or excellent, its depreciation of the importance of life's choices, its depreciation of truth ('*Redlichkeit*' – honesty with oneself and others). Nietzsche thinks that these are important sources of nihilism, from which we are suffering, and on which the philosopher should speak out.

But what positive remedies for this nihilism has Nietzsche to recommend? He speaks of a period of revolt and violence after which new values will emerge. We certainly seem to have gone through a period of much violence since his time, for which he has been held to some extent responsible. For him indeed there will always be struggle in the world; the question is whether it must be 'decadent' struggle. One notorious remark of Nietzsche's, frequently quoted, was: 'Even a Cesare Borgia rather than a Parsifal.' He most certainly did not regard the former as an exemplification of superman. This conception we must now try to elucidate.

Is superman a new product of possible future evolution totally unlike anything we can now imagine? Nietzsche's statement in *Zarathustra* – 'As ape is to man, a laughing-stock, a painful embarrassment, so will man be to superman' – has led some to this interpretation. And Nietzsche will not ignore that there is a factor of breeding, about which we understand little. But 'Darwin overlooked the factor of spirit'. Superman is an ethical conception, as the many discussions of his character show, a character grounded in self-discipline, capable of going under if need be, but above all who has found and lives by a system of values which is right for him, who is creative of value in himself and others. Goethe came near to Nietzsche's conception of superman; he said yes to the whole of life; so in another field did Julius Caesar. Nobility is his way of life instead of sinlessness: *'Viele Edlen und vielerlei Edlen bedarf es, dass es Adel gebe'* – 'many nobles and many kinds of nobles are needed, for there to be nobility in the world.'[7]

And 'eternal recurrence'? This seemingly odd idea, which has often been played down as a sign of his madness, represents his sense of the deep significance of ethical choice, in a world which is not to be devalued in the interests of an after-life. Would I choose this act if I knew I was to go on choosing it again and again for ever? Like the doctrine of *karma*, it raises insoluble problems about freedom and necessity. But the believer in *karma* does not feel absolved from the importance of choice now by the feeling that he is governed by the choices made in previous lives; nor does Nietzsche. Our choice becomes in some sense our destiny and this helps us to learn to love our destiny – *amor fati*. I think the oriental belief in *karma* serves much the same purpose as Nietzsche's belief in the eternal recurrence of the same events. What matters is that in this cyclical recurrence there should be some supermen; that is what justifies the whole.

We inevitably read Nietzsche in the age of the mass-media, and across the age of the dictators – an attempted reaction against mass-democracy. From his love of wit and verbal skill he certainly wrote some foolish things as well as others which show great insight and wisdom. What cannot, I think, be contended is that much of what he wrote is hopelessly dated, and of little interest to our generation.*

* N. Hartmann is a good exponent and corrective of Nietzsche's ethics (see *Ethics*, tr. S. Coit).

6

The Aftermath of German Idealism:
(2) Feuerbach and Marx

Karl Heinrich Marx (1818–83) is, for somewhat the same reasons
as Nietzsche, difficult for us to envisage as he was and as he
appeared to his contemporaries. For we inevitably read him across
the intervening years, during which he has become invoked as an
inspired prophet and teacher by almost half the world's population.
There has hardly been anyone who illustrates so forcibly Nietzsche's dictum that 'The quietest words bring about a storm;
thoughts that come on doves' feet change the course of the world'.[1]
The literature relating to Marx is even more overwhelming than
that on Nietzsche, and we can only steer a safe course through it
if we hold fast to two principles: to distinguish the various doctrines now officially entitled 'Marxism–Leninism' from what Marx
actually wrote; and to confine ourselves to the work of Marx as a
philosopher, by no means the least in the line of great German
philosophers. I shall therefore ignore purely economic questions,
questions of what is now called 'economics' and was already in
Marx's time recognized as a separate science of political economy,
such as the legitimacy of the conception of 'surplus value'.
Marx himself admitted as late as 1844 that he had not much
studied political economy as yet, when Engels sent him an essay

of his own on the subject. On the other hand he certainly did not regard sociology as a separate science; his views of class-structure in history are quite central to his philosophy, and can hardly be understood without a knowledge of his German predecessors.

In considering Nietzsche before Marx we have taken a liberty with historical chronology. Marx was already twenty-six when Nietzsche was born and had already written important articles; he died in the year Nietzsche wrote *Zarathustra*. We now have to go back almost a generation. My justification of this cavalier treatment of historical time is that Nietzsche's work is so much a sequel to, and revolt against, Schopenhauer's that they can hardly be separated. In this case, neglect of chronology does not cause much damage, for there is no evidence that Nietzsche was acquainted with any of Marx's work, and living in the unprofessorial atmosphere of Sils-Maria and Rapallo he had little interest in the academic controversies of old and young Hegelians (though the word *Übermensch* – 'superman' – as opposed to *Unmensch* – 'subman' – was used and perhaps coined by Marx). Nietzsche was influenced by the new, sociological, outlook, which had been a main theme of the French philosophers; but he did not, as Marx did, live through the revolutions of 1830, 1848 and the Paris Commune of 1871, which made these new ideas so exciting for Marx. A spiritual link between these two philosophers is the poet, Heinrich Heine, who was greatly admired by both, and who perhaps had it in him to understand two such diverse personalities.

Karl Marx was the son of a well-to-do Jewish lawyer of Trier in the Rhineland, who, without feeling any of Heine's strong reluctance, had become a nominal Christian on taking a post under the government. He was a man of liberal views, though a Prussian patriot, and not on the whole deeply concerned with the position of the Jews. His article, 'On the Jewish Question', written around 1844, maintains that Judaism and Christianity are much alike in that their true God is money; he treats the whole question of the Jews as one of social relations which the state cannot – as Hegel thought – settle by just enacting emancipation laws. It illustrates Marx's new thinking about 'civil' or 'bourgeois' society – the same

German term is used by Marx as by Hegel: '*bürgerliche Gesell-schaft*'. But how different is the connotation in English, according to how one translates this 'civil society' or 'bourgeois society'! This is a fundamental difficulty one encounters in translating Marx; through his work, the word '*bürgerlich*' gradually took on a pejorative sense.

Marx's youth coincided with the period between the revolutions of 1830 and 1848, which stirred the young men of his time and frightened most European governments. His student days were followed by a period of left-wing journalism, as editor of the *Rheinische Zeitung*, a Rhineland journal. This was soon suppressed by the Prussian government, and Marx migrated to Paris in 1843 and worked to establish a German-language paper there. In 1846 the Prussian government got him expelled from France and he had to move to Brussels. His period of exile in France was of great importance to him. He studied the French socialists at close quarters, and became acquainted with Heine and above all with his lifelong friend and loyal supporter, Engels. He met Engels in 1842 on the latter's going to take a post in his father's textile business in Manchester; two years later Engels presented him with a work on the condition of the working class in England, which had a powerful effect on Marx. His new intensive study of political economy was expressed in the economic and political manuscripts of 1844 published only in 1927, and in his work, *The Poverty of Philosophy* (*Misère de la Philosophie*), a polemical work written in French against Proudhon's all too simple equation – as Marx thought – of all property with theft.

'Socialism' at this epoch meant *French* socialism, in particular that of the Saint-Simonian and Fourierist communities, and of Louis Blanc. These communities were based upon an elaborate hierarchy and upon very doctrinaire principles concerning science and morals; fairly soon they were rent by factional disputes and broke up. It was Marx's experience in Paris that led him to his critique of what he called 'utopian socialism', and to the emphasis upon economic law and historical necessity which characterizes his later work.

Moved on to Brussels under Prussian government pressure upon the French, he founded in 1847 the Communist League – a title chosen in deliberate opposition to French 'socialism' – and he wrote along with Engels the *Communist Manifesto*, the most important single document of Marxism. Its opening words, 'A spectre is haunting Europe, the spectre of Communism,' are still a challenge in our own day.

In 1848, year of revolutions, he was able to return to Germany for a short while. The failure of the revolts in Germany led to his final exile in London, where he remained until his death. At first in real poverty, he was progressively helped by the loyal Engels, after Engels had succeeded to his father's business and to membership of the Manchester stock exchange. As is well known, the British Museum was the scene in which Marx wrote his greatest work, *Das Kapital*, of which the first volume was published in Hamburg in 1867. His practical experience with the International Working Men's Association (the 'First Internationale') and his quarrels with Lassalle belong to history. He remained on the whole more successful as a theorist than as a practical politician. His declining health was cheered by the devotion of his wife and by his love of literature, especially of Homer, the Greek dramatists and Shakespeare.

Engels continued the master's work after his death; it is often difficult, though necessary for the serious student, to distinguish his work from Marx's. It seems that Engels was responsible for coining the term 'dialectical materialism' and for extending this conception to the non-human world in his book, *Anti-Dühring*. (Similarly, the term 'historical materialism' seems to have been coined by Plekhanov, not Marx; but Marx certainly utilized similar conceptions in his mature work.) Engels was something of a soldier as well as a businessman, a much more genial, if more conventional personality than Marx.

The originality and vigour of the latter's thought cannot be denied, even when one discovers how much he built upon French sociology, British economics and German philosophy. The latter meant essentially that of Hegel and his successors. To Hegel he owed above all the notion of history as a process in which a rational order could be discovered. But for Hegel this rational order was to be discerned in two different processes: in the progressive 'objecti-fication' of spirit in the moral and legal order of society and state, with the struggle between states for leadership in world-history; but also in the progressive 'self-consciousness of absolute spirit' – the individual's realization of his identity with absolute spirit through art, religion and philosophy. In Hegel's system, as we saw, these two motifs, 'spirit objectified' and 'spirit absolute' becoming conscious of itself, are not perfectly assimilated – why indeed should great philosophers occur just at the climax of world history? Marx sought to bring these goals into connection. He also sought to bring what we called 'Hegel's pilgrimage', the *Phenomenology*, into connection with Hegel's goals. The former describes the progress of the individual, dissatisfied with ordinary sense-experience, through the stages described as stoicism, scepticism, unhappy consciousness, master and slave, guilt, self-estrangement, spiritual humbug, absolute freedom-and-terror. In this extraordinary account, Marx picked especially upon the phrase 'self-estrangement' or 'self-alienation' (*Selbstentfremdung*). Like Hegel, he found something radically wrong in man's situation; but unlike Hegel, for him it was something more than mere ignorance. It is in his work as at present organized that man is alienated from nature, from his specific human nature, from his own individuality and from his fellow-workers. Something must be done about this. 'Philosophers have interpreted the world in different ways, but the point is to change it' is his famous remark, from the *Theses on Feuerbach*.

Feuerbach (1804–72) had started from this dissatisfaction of man with his present lot, and had attributed this self-alienation of man to religion, 'the duplication of the world into a religious and a secular one'. His work, especially *The Essence of Christianity*, consists in explaining how this comes about, and in resolving the 'heavenly world' into its secular basis. God, whom man fears, is man's own projection; when he realizes this, man will no longer feel alienated in the present world. Feuerbach indeed turns Hegel upside down, making the course of world history not a self-revelation of absolute spirit, but an account of the changing ideas of individual men; theology is to become anthropology. 'Man is the beginning, end and centre of religions,' Feuerbach argues. But Marx writes that the fact that man establishes an independent realm in the clouds can only be explained by the cleavages and contradictions within this secular basis. Feuerbach, he says, does not see that religion itself is a social product, and that the individual whom he analyses belongs to a particular form of society. Social life is essentially practical.

Marx then takes up another Hegelian concept, that all man's works are an objectification (*Selbstentäusserung*) of himself – not however of a world-spirit or folk-spirit, but of the individual-in-his social-relations. Work is a process in which both man and nature participate; it ought to be something which

> he enjoys, as giving play to his bodily and mental powers. Whereas as soon as the division of labour begins, each man has a particular exclusive sphere of activity, which is forced upon him and which he cannot escape. He is a hunter, a shepherd, a fisherman, or a 'critical-critic', and must remain so, if he does not want to lose his means of livelihood. But in communist society, where no one has one exclusive sphere but each can become accomplished in anything he wishes, production as a whole is regulated by society and makes it possible for me to do one thing today and another tomorrow – hunt in the morning, fish in the afternoon, criticize after dinner according to my inclinations.

It has sometimes been – unfairly – maintained that this complete dilettantism is Marx's ideal of life. But his point is that the available forces of production – sheep, fishing-nets – give rise to social relations of production, and these regulate what shall be produced and how in a given society. These relations of production are the sources of dissatisfaction with the conditions of man's work; so that, he claims, in our present society most men feel no joy either in the product of their work or in their overcoming of nature, or in their humanity, or in the expression of their peculiar individuality. Surely this is fair observation and often true; can we do something about it? Is it inevitable? Is it wholly due to the particular relations of production which Marx was later to call 'capitalism'? Can the philosopher so change society that every man can take that pleasure in his work which the creative artist at his best does?

It is claimed by some interpreters that the doctrine of Marx's early works, with their concept of alienation, is wholly different from that of his later; and certainly there is more in his early works about man's situation, with an essentially humanistic ideal of how it might be transformed, and less about historical inevitability, and the absolute opposition between bourgeois and proletarian. I think it is a difference of emphasis rather than a complete reversal of doctrine, and that his conception of the state of communism as a goal – for example in the *Communist Manifesto*: 'from each according to his ability, to each according to his needs' – is essentially a freeing of man from the alienation described in his earlier work. Man's activity is to be completely free, once he has performed what *Das Kapital* describes as his 'socially necessary labour-time'. But the problem of defining what is socially necessary leaps to mind – to make his particular contribution to the space-race, for example?

I think the fact is that Marx absorbed Hegel's philosophy in two stages; the *Phenomenology* exercised a powerful influence upon him before he had very seriously studied the *Philosophy of Right*, with its theory of history and of the state. As for the *Logic* he tells us he first read it in 1857. After this, the notion of the inevitable dialectical process of history which we find in *Das Kapital* comes to the fore, and gives rise to those questions, about the inevitable course of economic fact and the superstructure of ideology reflecting it, that bother Marxists and their critics. For if the bourgeois, like the heathen of the hymn, 'in his blindness bows down to wood and stone', why lecture him? If the communist is bound to win by waiting, why risk his life?

The *Communist Manifesto* is a trumpet-call for a revolutionary effort – for which he feels the times are favourable. By the time he wrote *Das Kapital* he was fascinated by the idea of dialectic as a historical process, including Hegel's queer idea of 'the negation of the negation', by which a certain state of things inevitably turns into its opposite.

We may perhaps crudely characterize the three stages of Marx's thought as follows.

He is at first concerned with the psychological effect – the self-alienation – of man by reason of the division of labour which is enforced on him by society.

By the time of writing the *Communist Manifesto*, man has become 'the proletarian' – a term which seems to have been invented, or at least familiarized, by Marx's conservative enemy, Lorenz von Stein.[2] The proletarian is called the representative man, his future victory a victory of the 'universal class', not simply of one class over another. (Marx did not include the '*Lumpenproletariat*' – 'social scum' in the 1888 translation; 'drop-outs' – in the proletariat as 'representative men'.) His eloquent account of the achievements and the misdeeds of the bourgeois class, of their gradual reduction of all other classes to the condition of proletarians, is meant to open the eyes of all the revolutionary forces and spur them on to a life and death struggle with the bourgeois class. He concludes with a moral justification of the communist programme.

Finally, in *Das Kapital* the moral argument for this social change is quite submerged in a theory of inevitable change due to the 'dialectic' of history. The bourgeois class, because it will fail to get enough surplus value by any other means, will inevitably concentrate itself in great monopolies faced by an ever more uniform and more depressed proletariat – his theory of *Verelendung*, 'progressive misery'. Then, on the principle of the negation of the negation, the proletariat will seize the possessions of the bourgeois. The beliefs of individuals about all this are the inevitable result of their class position; the importance of class-consciousness is restricted to having a right understanding of where the process of history has got to – understanding whether the situation is a revolutionary one or not. The theory of increasing misery was thus important for Marx; the fact that it does not seem to have been verified, and the ways in which this is explained by Marxists – especially Lenin's theory of 'imperialism' – would lead us too far into economic theory.

As philosophy, what does Marx's contribution amount to? No doubt he has considerably helped to change 'the face of the world' – he claimed that this was the business of the philosopher, not just to interpret the world. However I think he would not have agreed that to change the world by any means whatever, such as naked force or deception, was the business of the philosopher. His philosophy is dominated by the main theme which exercised all German philosophers since Kant – to see together the data of our knowledge and reasonable belief on the one hand, and the demands of practice, especially of morality, on the other. At first he seems to come down on the same side as Fichte, in claiming that all knowledge, all reason, is to serve the requirements of morality. But in his mature work he follows Hegel in maintaining that morality is a phenomenon arising out of man's place in nature, society and history – morality, bourgeois and proletarian, is there to be understood as a sound fact.

Marx's recognition of the importance of the economic aspects of the individual's activity and of social history was a novel and vital contribution to thought. Equally novel was his emphasis on the fact that the individual's views and valuations are in the first instance derived from those of the group in which he grows up, and that from his identification of himself with one group or another arises the idea of 'class'; that this idea, though connected with the available 'forces of production', is partly subjective, deriving from the individual's felt identity of interests with members of one group in conflict with other groups, from feelings too of status and deference.

We may perhaps say that he overplayed both these novel and important propositions. First, in identifying economic motives with needs for material satisfactions. He was right in thinking that previous philosophers had much overlooked the importance of man's primary needs for food, drink and shelter, and in maintaining that the world in which these were to be found was in an important sense the real world, rather than the world of thoughts and images. But 'economizing' is a human activity which does not necessarily have to do with tangible things – there is an economics of time, for example; nor is the human being satisfied with the tangible and measurable only – Marx's own tirade against the alienation of labour proclaims this. Nor does recognition of the place of *economics* in history really imply anything about the constitution of non-human nature – 'materialism' in the original sense of that word. (But as we have seen, Marx was not much interested in this question, which he left to Engels.)

Second, his claim that all thought is ideology, determined by the class position of the thinker, is I believe, like some other philosophic doctrines such as solipsism, one that cannot be carried through consistently; it involves sawing off the branch on which you are sitting. This doctrine has given rise to an interesting new study, the sociology of knowledge – a comparative study of the things different groups of people believe. But it must be possible for individuals in spite of their class position – possible for Marx himself among others – to achieve truth in science and correct evaluation of the relative importance of the various goals of life.

Finally, it seems that his philosophy leads to an excessively doctrinaire view of politics which does not do justice to the facts. According to this, the correct thing to do at each juncture can be deduced from a knowledge of the dialectic of history. In particular, his doctrine that in the end 'the state is bound to wither away' implies a false view of the nature and true value of law, as a rational attempt to reconcile the divergent claims of men (unless one defines the term 'state' in an odd way, as an instrument of class coercion). Exacerbated as these divergences may be by our economic system, there is no reason to think that with the disappearance of capitalism all tensions between men would disappear. His philosophy of human nature is a 'clean slate' philosophy, assuming (with Locke who first suggested the idea) that the individual's character is entirely the product of his environment; heredity does not come into it. But this does not seem to be true.

Like every important philosophy, it aims to give us a tentative view of the most general relations between nature, man, history, culture. Understanding of his philosophy is necessary for the great task of our time – of finding ways in which the communist and non-communist halves of the world can live together and contribute to one another – whether 'capitalism', 'communism' or something unimaginably different from either is destined to prevail in the end. Of this we shall have to say something in a later chapter. For as the American, George Kennan, wrote, what divides them is not really 'a diagreement about what economic arrangements are most productive, but about what is most important'.*

We need to recognize that there is a more humanistic and a less humanistic aspect in Marxist philosophy. Marx was in many ways a child of the Enlightenment, with a personal admiration for classical humanism, eager to deliver man from a state of society in which he could not develop his natural powers to the full. His humanism differs indeed from that of Goethe, owing to the importance he assigns to work and to the need for change. It is an ideal which non-proletarians can share, and discussion of the means of realizing it is possible. On the other hand he portrays a class-conflict so universal and ceaseless that it is hard to see how any means of winning the struggle can be ruled out. The assertion that there can be some standards, e.g. of truthfulness or fidelity, common to bourgeois and proletarian is on this view just a piece of bourgeois ideology. The view of some of his following of the absolute wickedness of the capitalist leads to a position like that of the medieval Church, where 'no faith is to be kept with heretics', and certainly makes cooperation difficult. It seems certain that Marx was not right in maintaining that all classes result from economic struggle, or that the only important historical groupings are bourgeois and proletariat. He was asserting as a universal truth of social history a generalization which was true only of Western Europe in the latter half of the nineteenth century. Anyone basing his observations on, e.g. the formation of classes and ideological groups in late Antiquity would come to very different conclusions.

* *Foreign Affairs*, January 1960.

7
Freud

Was Sigmund Freud a philosopher? Or was he simply a practising physician who incidentally threw out some interesting philosophical ideas, as many practitioners of this highly philosophical art have done? If philosophy, is, as I think, the invention or discovery of thought-forms which bear upon the most important matters 'with the fewest presuppositions', then I have no doubt that he must count as a philosopher, who could not possibly be omitted even from such a work as this. Notions such as 'the unconscious', 'repression', 'libido' or sexuality in the wide sense it has now acquired; dreams, mistakes, jokes as significant of unconscious attitudes – these have become common currency of our culture. No one, with the possible exception of Marx, has so greatly influenced the way we think of – and therefore the way we observe – our fellow men.

And his work must certainly be reckoned as part of the German tradition, although like that of Wittgenstein its influence in the English-speaking countries has probably been greater. His conception of the unconscious is largely derived from Eduard von Hartmann,[1] a pupil of Schopenhauer, the latter being perhaps the first to stress the enormous philosophical importance of sexuality. His concept of the Id and much else of his later philosophy derives from Nietzsche, and he shows a great love of German literature, especially of Goethe and Heine.

Freud was anything but a mere practitioner, uninterested in the philosophical aspects of his work. In 1896 he wrote: 'When I was young, the only thing I longed for was philosophical knowledge'; and his last work, the *New Introductory Lectures*, is decidedly philosophical, concluding with a chapter entitled 'A philosophy of life'. This concern also finds notable expression in his short but wide-ranging work, *Civilization and its Discontents*, in which he takes a fairly positive attitude towards philosophy, maintaining that its method is essentially that of science, only that it is apt to claim to run ahead too fast and at times to rely upon intuition to secure eternal truth. Such a view of philosophy would be widely rejected today.

Yet, as in the case of Marx, it is not easy to know how to fit him into such a work as this. In the first place, there is already an immense literature about him, both popular and scientific, both scholarly and tendentious, and some of it even grossly unfair. Second, there arises, as with Marx, the problem of his followers, both approved and heretical; only in his case there is only an International Psycho-Analytical Association, not a government, to maintain the canon of orthodoxy. In the present chapter we shall have to ignore the disciples, both orthodox and heretical. It is clear that we must omit all discussion of his therapeutic methods, upon which there are excellent historical and critical accounts to be had. Their value has been a good deal criticized in our day, e.g. by Eysenck, whereas Freud's disciples claim that this is partly due to their being applied in unsuitable cases – Freud himself is very clear about the limits of their proper application.[2] To some extent, too, it is a matter of judgement what conceptions are to be regarded as matters of therapeutic technique, and which on the other hand belong to his general view of the anatomy of the personality, its development, its relation to its environment, natural and social. Many popular notions, such as 'the Oedipus complex', or 'penis-envy', I shall regard as belonging to the former category, of psychotherapeutic technique rather than of general philosophy. Even so, as Wollheim says, by the breadth and audacity of his speculations he revolutionized the thought, the lives and the imagination of an age.

Freud was born in a remote village of Moravia in 1856, and in the 1860s his family settled in Vienna, where he studied medicine at the university and made the acquaintance of Breuer, in partnership with whom all his early work was done. In 1885-6 he worked in Paris under Charcot, the first European doctor to employ hypnosis – though rather as a means of diagnosing symptoms which were 'hysterical' than as a therapy. The idea that it might be used as a therapy by 'abreaction' was probably contributed by Breuer, though both men worked closely together. 1896 saw the publication of their first important work, and the first use of the term 'psycho-analysis'. In 1900 his major work, *The Interpretation of Dreams*, was published. In 1915-17 the *Introductory Lectures on Psycho-Analysis* were given in the University of Vienna. Meantime Breuer had dissociated himself from Freud, on the issue of infantile sexuality; Adler left him in 1912; he had begun to find some resonance for his ideas in the Zurich school of Bleuler and Jung; the latter went his own way in 1912. In 1919 Freud published *Beyond the Pleasure-Principle*, which was in many ways a turning-point in his philosophy. In 1933 his books were burned in Berlin. In 1938 he removed to London where he died the next year, after sixteen years of severe illness (cancer) during which he carried on his work, often in great pain. He was a philosopher whose life decidedly conformed with his beliefs.

His philosophical importance consists in the novel view which he advanced regarding the structure of the mind in relation to that of the body (if we should so speak), and its social consequences. It is easy – and foolish – to make fun of some of the terms he employed; such as 'Superego' and 'Id' (*das Es*). He was an imaginative man, with a great sense for the drama of life, and such figurative expressions came naturally to him. One remarkable feature of his work is that he was always in principle a scientist in the nineteenth-century sense, convinced that a causal explanation in terms of material events would always in the end be found. And yet he was the first to break with the purely neurological conception of psychiatry which dominated his contemporaries, and to attempt to explain some strictly physical symptoms such as blindness or lameness in strictly psychical terms of 'purpose' and 'conflict' – indeed in terms which take their meaning from social life, as 'conflict', 'repression' and 'censorship' do. Hardly any of his theories are susceptible of strictly scientific proof, because of the impossibility of experiment on human beings and the difficulty of finding control-groups. He remained convinced that neurology would provide proof of them some day. His very great merit was his insight that the mental manifests itself in bodily symptoms, in many tricks of speech and behaviour, which are not in any ordinary sense conscious. For behaviour is not a strictly physical concept at all, as the new science of animal ethology has made evident in our own time.

Now, much of the mental can become conscious at any time, if suitable circumstances occur – this component he was to label the 'pre-conscious'. But he demonstrated that much can only be made conscious by means of special techniques, such as hypnotic trance or 'free association', and, as he later thought, through interpretation of dreams; and that such bringing of the unconscious into consciousness was almost always accompanied by outbursts of emotion. Indeed his great advance on his predecessors was the recognition that it is instincts (*Triebe*, 'drives'*) rather than memories which are repressed. The alleged memories which his patients recovered often turned out to be fictitious – this was a major cause of Jung's secession from Freud. Mind then must be thought of as a place of conflict – a notion, we might say not very different from that of Plato's *Phaedrus*, with its two horses representing instinct and reason. Freud, however, viewing the matter from the point of view of a neurologist, asked himself what is the source of the repressing energy, if instincts are repressed by the reason, and how on balance it is conserved – for he always believed in what Kohler was later to call 'isomorphism', a correspondence of some kind between mind and brain.

According to his first model then, conflict was always between what he called the 'pleasure-principle' and the 'reality-principle'.

---

* A translation difficulty, for 'instinct' in English normally implies something inherited, and shared with animals; hence the introduction of the word '*drive*'.

The Ego is pushed one way by an inexorable demand for the maximum satisfaction of instincts or drives, and pushed in the opposite direction owing to the pain incurred through natural or social facts when it attempts this gratification. In consequence, fulfilment of some of the most urgent drives, sex among them, will be obstructed, or manifest itself in odd ways, hysterical or neurotic. (Pavlov was to show that animals can be brought into a quasi-neurotic condition by suitably-conflicting stimuli, a fact which is given as proof of some assertions of psycho-analysis.)

An outstanding feature of Freud's earlier theory was that such a process of repression into unconsciousness must start with the birth of the individual – not necessarily with some later 'trauma' (injury) – and be bound up with the nature of the relation of child to mother, father, brothers and sisters. He had already come to the conclusion that the sex instinct was extremely powerful, and the one most often repressed in later life. He therefore was led greatly to extend the usual sense of the word 'sexuality' to cover phenomena which manifested themselves at all ages from infancy onwards – anal, oral, phallic, genital eroticism, narcissism and the like. Now this is a matter of semantics – a question of whether this extension of the meaning of this word is illuminating or misleading. It has no bearing upon the question whether Freud supposed that sex drive was a universal cause of all psychical developments; and even less upon the question whether he advocated complete freedom from all sexual repression as a panacea for all ills. Neither of these propositions, though widely held, is true. His wider use of the word 'sexuality' led to his being accused of pansexualism, for which there is no justification either as characterizing his theory or his practice.

The second phase of Freud's development, which starts with *Beyond the Pleasure-Principle* (1919), is philosophically much the most interesting. In it he introduces an 'anatomy of the personality' – of which he gives a diagram in *New Introductory Lectures*. It consists of Ego, Id and – a new concept – Superego. He further conceives the dynamics of the whole as a conflict between two forces, which he names *Eros* and *Thanatos* (from the Greek for 'death').

He now makes a sharp distinction between repression of drives that is due to natural circumstances and that which is due to social causes. This is due to his further study of anxiety, topic of so much later philosophy. Freud now recognizes three types:[3] normal anxiety, in face of a real danger; neurotic anxiety, totally lacking a foundation in reality; and what he calls moral anxiety, related to, but out of all proportion to, some social requirement, such as cleanliness or truth-telling. The latter gives rise to guilt-feelings. Through alleged processes of childhood which we need not follow here, the social retaliation which results from unlimited satisfaction of the individual's drives is 'introjected' – internalized – in what he now calls the Superego. He holds it on the whole true, and the simplest assumption, that it is essentially the aggressive drives and their punishment which are internalized in the Superego, and give rise to moral anxiety. This concept of the Superego evidently corresponds to a great extent with the traditional concept of 'conscience', but whereas this was always associated with rationality and a true estimation of requirements, Freud wants to maintain that it is often opposed to the rational insights of the Ego, and to indicate the source of its powers – in the aggressive instincts of the Id.

The Superego is never more than partly conscious; its repressions can be brought into consciousness only by special techniques. It is felt by the Ego as a special kind of restriction upon its freedom, often more oppressive than more direct natural and social restrictions. It may be a source of neurosis, especially of obsessional neurosis, and is always a major factor for the understanding both of individual development and of social life.

His great innovation in his second period is to recognize the originality and universality of a drive involving aggression against others, and to claim that it is a drive for destruction; further, that it can be turned against oneself (compare Nietzsche's: 'You sheep, you are alone to blame'). It is universal, not a perversion of sex drive, as sadism is. The most striking feature of the new doctrine is that moral self-aggression – a purely psychic concept – is what is responsible in the end for the physical death of the individual; hence the name *Thanatos*. This is of course Buddhist philosophy:

'sense-fields→contact→feeling→craving→grasping→becoming→ birth→decay-and-death (the links of conditioned co-production)'.[4] It is unlikely that Freud derived it from this source. There is of course physical evidence for the view that some cells of the body, especially of the brain, start to die as soon as it is born and do not regenerate, and we may well think that there are psychic factors which promote or postpone death. Hardly anyone however has followed Freud in this doctrine, that moral self-aggression or sense of guilt is the sole or even the overriding answer to the riddle of the nature of death. It is in my view a genuine philosophical question, on which both semantic clarification and experiment are in place. The phenomenon of oppressive and apparently inexplicable sense of guilt is also one of genuine philosophical importance.

Opposed now to the death drive, Eros, erotic drive, takes on a much broader significance than Freud had given even to the sex drive. Rooted in a kernel of sexuality, Eros now represents the totality of all human drives whose outcome is constructive and socially binding. Well-directed, sexuality or Eros expands into stable mutual love, friendship, order, love of beauty, art, even science. It is the root of all that is worth while in culture and civilization. It may be true that Freud had no 'articulated social theory or ethic' (Wollheim); still he thought a good deal about this, and his views in *Civilization and its Discontents* and *The Future of an Illusion* are well worth consideration.

He has no doubt that culture, by which he means a fairly complex modern social order, is worth while, for it alone makes possible the expansion of Eros which we have described, and keeps destructive Thanatos within bounds. But its costs in terms of renunciation of the unlimited satisfaction of individual drives are great. To prevent mutual destruction, much forcible repression of the individual's aggressive drives is necessary, and yet they cannot be dispensed with, for the defence of both the individual and of his society. And this involves setting limitations upon the satisfaction of many other drives which would lead to aggression and mutual destruction – upon the sex drive among others. What he calls 'rational judgement' on how much self-restriction is necessary – the achievement of a morality that is free from anxiety

– is in his view possible only for the few. 'Sublimation', the diversion of drives to other, innocuous, objects is possible only to a limited extent. Following Schopenhauer, he holds that pleasure in art is often a substitute for satisfaction with cruder types of pleasure, but again, only to a limited extent. He examines at some length the Marxist utopian theory that all social troubles could be abolished by the abolition of property in the means of production, and concludes that it is but a dream – destructive aggression due to sex-rivalry is at least as powerful a motive as rivalry due to differences of power and wealth. It is as impossible to do without government by a minority as to do without coercion in the work of civilization, for

> the masses are lazy and unintelligent, they have no love for instinctual renunciation, and are not to be convinced of its inevitability by argument . . . All is well if leaders are people of superior insight into what constitutes the necessities of life, people who have attained the height of mastering their own instinctual wishes . . . But men are not naturally fond of work, and arguments are of no avail against their passions.[5]

What about religion? – 'clearly religion has contributed much towards restraining the asocial instincts, but still not enough.' It does not seem to have reconciled the majority of mankind to life, and made them loyal supporters of civilization. People were certainly not more moral in times when religion reigned undisputed. In the case of the Christian religion, 'the command "to love one's neighbour as oneself" is not only impossible to carry out but destructive of genuine love and friendship'. But the chief case against religion is that it will be found out to be a fraud in the end; 'the voice of understanding is a soft one, but it does not rest until it has gained a hearing.'

Freud is a philosopher in the great tradition of the Enlightenment. Although he admits that 'the theory of the instincts is, as it were, our mythology; the instincts are mythical beings', he did not think much about the nature of mythology (it might be argued that on the contrary Jung lost himself in a mythology that he claimed was psychologically true).

Freud always refused to be a moralist, to recommend a morality to his patients (like Horney); he claimed only to show them themselves, and let them find an individual morality appropriate to themselves, if they could. Still less did he claim to be a social prophet. 'Nor does psychoanalysis,' he concludes, 'create a philosophy of life. It subscribes to the scientific philosophy, in the emphasis it lays on the real world, limiting itself to truth and rejecting illusions.' This may not be the whole, but surely it represents a great part of the traditional aim of philosophy.

The most serious criticism of his philosophy is that it ignores the possibility that differences of culture may be causative; that the process of repression which he describes may be typical of a patriarchal society such as he was acquainted with, but not of a matriarchal society. It is true that these great differences of cultures only began to be explored in the latter years of his life; however the German tradition since Herder was well aware of its importance. But Freud was essentially the biologist, and regarded his whole apparatus of 'instincts' as being just as universal as the apparatus of bodily organs. As Habermas well observes,* Freud believed himself to be discovering causal laws that would one day be verified by neurology; but his real originality lay in a work of re-interpretation – of dreams, alleged memories, inadvertent actions – in such a way as to make clear to the patient that his original, conscious interpretation was false, and what the reasons were for this false interpretation.

* See p. 162.

8

Linguistic Philosophy:
Frege, the Vienna Circle,
Wittgenstein and Dilthey

While in England around the turn of the century philosophical debate centred around the opposition of 'absolute idealism' and various sorts of realism, in Germany debate was rather between those concerned with the historical and cultural aspects of Hegel's philosophy and those who represented a 'back-to-Kant' movement. The former were represented by Dilthey and the so-called south-west German school, of which the most important representative was Max Weber. The latter, influenced by Comte, were especially concerned to distinguish, and exclude, metaphysics from science. Both groups therefore became much concerned with the nature of language, though from different points of view; and the latter, 'positivistic', group were divided between those mainly concerned with the language of mathematics and those primarily interested in the language of physical science. Both had an enormous influence upon the British tradition, though at different times and by different routes.

The first question to exercise these German philosophers was that of the kinship between ordinary language and mathematical symbolism. Leibniz had already noted that mathematics had devised a system of symbols which is intelligible to persons of the most diverse mother-tongues. He thought it should therefore be possible to construct a universal language on the basis of a similar symbolism; as he said, instead of arguing 'let us calculate!' Hitherto, following Plato and Descartes, mathematics had been thought of as concerned with a special sort of ideal – entities like perfect circles – rather than as a special way of talking about ordinary things in this world, for special purposes. With the work on alternative geometries by Lobachevsky in 1855, and the development of the different types of transfinite numbers by Dedekind and Cantor in the latter half of the nineteenth century, the idea emerged that mathematical symbolism might provide various different ways of speaking about the world. This idea was encouraged in England by Boole (1816–64) demonstrating that the logical relations on which ordinary speech relies could be expressed in mathematical symbolism.

But the conception of mathematics as a language, and as perhaps exhibiting the true nature of language, and so clearing up philosophical puzzles, derives from *Gottlob Frege* (1848–1925). After first developing a 'conceptual language' (*Begriffssprache*) in the manner of Leibniz, in 1879 he began, in his subsequent works, especially in *On Sense and Reference*, to explain the necessary relations between names and concepts, propositions and what they refer to, establishing far more clearly than anyone before him had done what it is for a proposition to be meaningful, and what are the conditions for it to be true. He maintained that in arithmetic we can and do refer to numbers, which are objects, although not in space and time. Philosophy could and should develop a purified language, such that logical mistakes in the use of it would be impossible. Frege's work exercised an enormous fascination upon Bertrand Russell, who at one time conceived his main task as that of developing a perfect language – a symbolism in which any logical error would be immediately seen to be such. But what is a perfect language? This was a theme that was to exercise the philosophers of the British tradition for a generation, though it did not attract so much attention in Germany. (The fact that a language is something necessarily social, since it must involve applying rules acceptable to more than one person, remained unremarked until demonstrated by Dilthey and in the later works of Wittgenstein.) Frege's ideas were combined by Bertrand Russell with Hume's psychology to form Russell's own characteristic 'philosophy of logical atomism'.

The second attempt to develop a language, but one in which no mistakes of fact could be stated without our noticing it, because it would be freed from unclear metaphysical phraseology, derives from *Ernst Mach* (1838–1916). Its scene was Vienna. Mach was a philosophically-interested physicist, whose aim was to purify the language of physics from all such conceptions as 'atoms', 'force', 'energy', 'cause', 'absolute space and time' – i.e. from all conceptions that do not refer directly to individual experiences. Scientific language should be only a re-description of experience, not an, explanation; it should attempt merely to state, in terms of mathematical functions, how such experiences are related to one another e.g. when I experience a body freely falling. Hypotheses, or 'new rules' as he preferred to call them, must be stated in terms of the particular tests which – as we usually say – confirm them, and are to be regarded as true after a sufficient number of such tests. This view of language, which claimed that we should only state what is definitely testable by experiences, which could in principle be listed, is the germ of the famous verification principle, the basis of the movement called by its adherents 'logical positivism' – of which more later.

In 1907 the *Verein Ernst Mach* was started in Vienna to promote and develop his ideas, by a number of philosophers who later became notable; and when in 1922 Moritz Schlick succeeded to Mach's professorship, they became known as the Vienna Circle. It comprised among others Schlick, who was by training a physicist; Neurath, an economist; Carnap, a mathematician pupil of Frege; and the distinguished philosophers, Waismann, Popper, Gödel, and Reichenbach. (The actual term 'Vienna Circle' – '*Wiener Kreis*' – seems however to have been first used in 1929.) They were all agreed upon the central truth of Mach's principle that 'the meaning of any statement consists in the facts of experience that verify it.' Unless these can be indicated, the statement is meaningless (*unsinnig*). They were a remarkable body of men, many of whom later migrated to England or the United States and published their most notable works there. But in the period from 1922 onwards they were all concerned in trying to give a more rigorous formulation to the verification principle.

But divergences between them soon appeared, both as to the truth of the verification principle – was it itself verifiable?; was it self-evident?; was it a scoial rule? – and as to the kind of experiences which could verify statements. This new principle for purifying language of all confused and nonsensical statements gave rise to illuminating differences. Schlick, the leader of the Circle until he was shot by one of his female students, maintained that the relevant experiences were states of mind, sights, sounds and smells, states of my mind and of other minds. But then, is there not something essentially private about these; can I know that a note as I hear it corresponds exactly with what another hears simultaneously? Because of this element of incommunicable private enjoyment (*Erlebnis*) the verifying fact could only be one of structure, e.g. of the relative position of two different notes in the scale; this could be common to both experiences – but can I be sure even of that?

This did not satisfy two other members of the group, Neurath and Carnap. These considered that the fact which made the statement true must be public and accessible to anyone. So the former developed the theory that the ultimate facts were given in so-called protocol-statements, such as: 'At 3.20 pm *Otto said that* he heard middle C sounded, or felt a toothache.' Such statements did reflect public facts, certainly, but what was said might be quite untrue. Carnap therefore developed a view of language known as 'physicalism', according to which the only ultimate language is the language of physics, and the ultimate facts are such as can be described as 'The body called Otto is in a state of note-hearing – or green-seeing.' He purported to explain how all ordinary statements can be reduced to such statements of physical events; while all philosophical statements such as 'a person has a mind' were not about facts but about the usage of the *words* 'person' and 'mind'.

As he maintained in his influential book, *The Logical Syntax of Language*, to demonstrate this is the sole legitimate purpose of philosophy; philosophy may at best recommend how words should be used in a language which is to be perfectly meaningful. We cannot, in such a work as this, follow through the elaborate technical discussions about translatability to which this gave rise, especially since the working out of all the consequences of this theory took place mainly in England and America. The movement entitled Logical Positivism belongs rather to the British than to the German tradition; it was transmitted to England by Alfred Ayer (b. 1910) through his prodigiously successful book *Language, Truth and Logic* (1936). It did not cause much of a stir in Germany, largely for historical reasons extraneous to philosophy; and after 1933 most of its distinguished exponents went into enforced or voluntary exile. Many produced works of great distinction; on the whole, they abandoned the ideal of a perfect language, and explored the merits of different sorts of language (Waismann), or rejected the Viennese doctrine that there must be *some* absolutely certain basic propositions in the language of science. Popper wrote: 'All science is a matter of sinking piles in a marsh' – together they stand up though not a single one would stand up by itself.[1]

Logical positivism was also seen in England as a development of the early work of Ludwig Wittgenstein. He never belonged to the Vienna Circle, although he was in touch with it, especially through his friend, Friedrich Waismann. But during the period we have been discussing he was not much concerned with questions of academic philosophy. While he was greatly influenced by the English tradition through Bertrand Russell, as we shall see, he belongs on the whole decidedly to the German tradition, all his major works being written in German, and Schopenhauer being an early and a major influence in his life. But his work is of such originality that it cannot readily be put in one of the traditional pigeon-holes.

Ludwig Wittgenstein (1889–1951) resembled Leibniz in being a man of an extraordinary variety of talents. He excelled as mathematician, engineer, musician, sculptor, and as a writer of beautiful

German. Unlike Leibniz, however, he was a man of extraordinary concentration upon the task which a passionate devotion to the discovery of truth seemed to lay upon him. His life is relevant in the highest degree to the character of his philosophy. Son of a wealthy and extremely enterprizing industrialist, he was trained as an engineer in Berlin, and went to Manchester in 1909 to complete his studies. There he became acquainted with the early work of Russell, determined, at the age of twenty-two, to go to Cambridge to study under him, and was admitted to Trinity College in 1912. Within two years however the First World War broke out, and he immediately returned to Austria, where he served as an officer throughout the war, first on the eastern, then on the southern front, before being taken prisoner and interned by the Italians. During his internment he wrote his only major work published during his lifetime, the *Logisch-Philosophische Abhandlung*, published in German in 1921, in English translation, as *Tractatus Logico-Philosophicus*, in 1922. (It is usually cited as the *Tractatus*.) At the end of the war he sent the manuscript to Bertrand Russell, who recognized its merits while disagreeing with its general trend.

But just then Wittgenstein felt unable to continue with philosophy – we may bear in mind the terrible economic situation of Austria at the time. He gave away the rest of his wealth – in 1914 he had already given most of it to support the poet Rilke – and took a post as a primary schoolteacher in several remote Austrian villages; then as a gardener in a monastery. During this period he built a much-admired house in Vienna for his sister. Without acknowledging any conventional religion, his manner of life was at all times extremely ascetic; he spent much of his time in a remote hut in Norway, later in one he built for himself on the coast of Galway. In Cambridge his Fellow's room was furnished with a table and two kitchen chairs. During the Second World War he worked as a hospital orderly. His life, we may judge from the memoirs of von Wright and Malcolm, was devoted, like that of Socrates and Spinoza, to an ethical ideal of which he would say little and which he included in 'the mystical' of which – as he tells us at the end of the *Tractatus* – nothing can be said. His works are the outcome of, yet by no means a clue to, the underlying motives of his life. On his return to Cambridge in 1929, first as Research Fellow, later as Professor, his lectures were quite unique, described as a 'visible struggle with his thoughts'. On the whole he detested Cambridge, and made no effort to conceal the fact. Such was the Austrian–German who has been the greatest single influence upon British philosophy in our time.

So wide is the gap between his early work the *Tractatus*, and his later work, the *Philosophical Investigations*, written, it seems, between about 1933 and 1949 and published in England in 1953 in parallel columns of German and English, that many have spoken of his 'two philosophies'. But increasingly a connection has been seen in the efforts of the two works to make clear to us the power and the limits of language as a means of disclosing reality. Each book is dominated by a certain simile: in the first book he sees language as a system of pictures, each mirroring an item of reality; in the second he sees it as a system of games which we play with reality.

In the *Tractatus* Wittgenstein starts from the position that it is nonsensical to argue, as for example Bradley and Russell were then doing, first about what reality is like in itself, a seamless whole or a lot of atoms, and then about whether our statements about it are true. For all the time we are utilizing language. So that somewhere there must be a non-linguistic relation between our statements and the facts they purport to state. This can only be a relation which he describes as 'picturing' or 'showing'. Since many statements, notably false statements and indefinite ones – e.g. about all future babies – plainly do not picture facts, there must be some simple 'objects' as he calls them, which are 'pictured' or 'shown' by some elementary propositions, in terms of which all other propositions about more complex states of affairs (*Sachverhalte*) can be explained. He gives a method (truth-table logic) by which this can be done.

As to whether these simple objects were physical (as Carnap maintained) or sense-data and images (as Russell maintained), there was much argument among critics, but it seems clear that Wittgenstein refused to commit himself. Difficulties at once arose about the simplicity of the basic propositions – whether, e.g. 'This box is black' could be further split, and just how it 'showed' or reflected a fact. These are technical questions of logic. But two consequences were philosophically more important. The first is what has been called his 'finitism'. If, as he says, the whole of logical space is filled with particular facts, any general propositon must be 'unpacked' (as was said) into a finite number of propositions, each showing a definite fact; but this does not seem to be the case with propositions asserting scientific laws. If it were really taken as a rule by scientists, it would stultify the progress of science, which wants to make quite general – if tentative – assertions about all facts of a kind. And the second is the doctrine that all propositions that cannot be thus unpacked are either tautologies or nonsensical, not even false – the latter including all propositions about morality, art and religion, and most of the propositions of traditional philosophy. He was prepared to say that some of the latter were important nonsense, but still, nonsense. 'Of that of which one cannot speak, one must be silent.'

But he meant: 'Of that of which one cannot speak in this type of language.' Already by 1933, according to von Wright, he was feeling that this view of language was too restrictive – though it was recognized that the *Tractatus* gave us new insights into the possible logical and semantic relations upon which language is built up. In fact men do contrive to speak intelligibly about the many matters he had ruled out as nonsensical.

The *Tractatus* gives the impression of a neat design in which its seven main propositions, each with its numbered sub-propositions, fit together exactly like pieces in a jigsaw puzzle, without any digressions or concessions to the reader. Very different is the method of the *Philosophical Investigations*. It consists of 784 questions put to the reader in separate paragraphs in what appears at first sight to be a random order. Each paragraph consists of what people either do say or might say in various concrete situations of life. It is not easy to find conclusions as to what Wittgenstein himself thought on the subject of the paragraph; he is determined that the reader shall philosophize for himself on these data.*

* In all, eight volumes of disconnected 'remarks', in a more or less random order, have been published.

The *Philosophical Investigations* are difficult to summarize because unlike the *Tractatus* they are so unsystematic; nevertheless some connected themes can be detected by the attentive reader. The whole is dominated by the basic simile of language as an aggregate of many different social games played with reality. Its main theses can be summarized in the two slogans: 'The speaking of a language is part of an activity or a form of life';[2] and 'Every sentence in our language is in order as it is.'[3] As for the multitude of language-games he lists:

> Giving and obeying orders
> Describing an object, giving its measurements
> Constructing an object from a description
> Reporting an event
> Speculating about an event
> Forming and testing an hypothesis
> Presenting the result of an experiment
> Making up a story and reading it
> Play-acting
> Singing catches
> Guessing riddles
> Making a joke; telling it
> Solving a problem in practical arithmetic
> Translating from one language into another
> Asking, thanking, cursing, greeting, praying

– all these are as much part of our natural history as walking, eating drinking, playing.

After discussing the variety of language-games there are, he goes on to discuss those we play in relation to pain, to thinking, imagining, understanding, giving reasons for action, will, intention, seeing, believing, seeing aspects in ambiguous diagrams (like the cube and the cornice). The facts to which he draws attention in all this are generally novel, and the insights he propounds extremely original. For example, how we dispose of various kinds of pretence, 'for lying is also a language-game'; how we judge that someone is reading; why it makes sense to say that an animal is in pain, but not that the stove is in pain; the difference between intending and predicting that my arm will go up. It may well be said that this is not philosophy, only raw material for philosophy; but philosophy, he maintains, is 'assembling reminders for a particular purpose'.[4] When we thoroughly understand the rules of the particular language-game which we are playing 'philosophical problems should *completely* disappear'. 'There is not a philosophical method, though there are different methods, like different therapies.'[5] Philosophy can only clear up confusions, and confusions to which philosophers are particularly liable, owing to their desire to generalize – e.g. to use the word 'image' both of works of art and in description of dreams. Philosophy for him is a therapy, though more so for his pupil, J. Wisdom.

This brings us to the other main feature of *Philosophical Investigations*: the assertion that there is only a remote family resemblance between language-games, and that each game is in order as it is – e.g. in 'This room is *full*', the meaning and truth is entirely dependent on the context, physical, social, and so on, in which it is used. But here he goes to the opposite extreme from the *Tractatus*, and admits, for example, that assertions within the language-games of witchcraft or scientology are perfectly in order as they are, and that their truth may not be criticized from any outside standpoint. This seems to go too far, in treating all language-games as, so to say, on a par with one another; some are surely more fundamental than others, and it may well be that they have a common root, as Chomsky thinks. In any case, language is rather too serious a matter to be completely described as a series of games. Surely there are significant relations between the language-games of psychology, morality, art, which a wide-ranging philosophy may enable us to discern. F. Waismann spoke of 'language-strata', each with its appropriate logic. Some may be basic for an understanding of all the rest, a subject developed by Professor Strawson in our own day: we must be able to recognize 'the same individuals' in order to speak at all.

Wittgenstein's work has been far more influential in the English-speaking than in the German-speaking countries. His affinities with the English tradition of Hume and Russell have been deliberately ignored in the present work; the affinity sometimes suggested between his outlook and that of Moore seems to the present writer very questionable. As will be suggested, he has a good deal in common with the Existentialist philosophers of the German tradition. His life is a remarkable example of the way in which philosophers brought up in different traditions – in spite of some periods of blank failure to understand what each other were about – can fruitfully cooperate.

> Confucius was asked, if he had to govern the nation, what he would do first. He replied: 'Correct language. If language is not correct, then what is said is not what is meant; if what is said is not really meant, then what ought to be done remains undone; if what ought to be done remains undone, morals and art will deteriorate, justice will go astray; if justice goes astray, the people stand about in helpless confusion. Hence there must be no indifference about what is said; this matters above everything.'[6]

In any discussion of language, there is another German philosopher who must be mentioned, though he did not regard himself as concerned just with language but with the means of social communication generally, and the strikingly different uses to which they are put in the natural sciences on the one hand and the human sciences (*Geisteswissenschaften*) on the other. *Wilhelm Dilthey* (1833–1911) pointed out that we already have well-developed techniques for interpreting law or an ancient chronicler; and that these are different from the usual techniques of the natural sciences. The former depend upon the presumption that the law or historical statement is meaningful within a given human society; it will depend upon the current understanding of language, as well as upon the practices of the society. He therefore distinguished 'hermeneutics' (interpretation) of the human sciences from 'explanation' in the natural sciences; and emphasized that this interpretation is a matter not of psychology (as he originally thought) but of understanding objective happenings, such as speech, work, transactions.

From this point he went on to explore the problems of social sciences, such as economics, which seem to involve features of natural causal explanation *and* humanistic interpretation. Into these problems – some of the most important in our day – we cannot at present follow him. But it is likely that he influenced the later Wittgenstein; and certain that he influenced Freud and the Frankfurt school.

Although Schleiermacher (1768–1834) invented the word, which he used purely with reference to biblical interpretation, Dilthey can be regarded as the founder of 'hermeneutics', which has come to play an important part in the philosophical thought of our time. It may be taken to cover 'the systematic study of the methods of interpreting anything known to be or considered as a human artefact'. Originally confined to the study of texts in a known language, it was applied by Dilthey to the systematic methods of interpretation employed in all the humanistic sciences, such as law and history. But this was bound to raise such questions as: how far are the same methods applicable to objects found by archaeologists, to customs strange to us discovered by anthropologists, to works of plastic and graphic art – and indeed to the texts of the philosophers themselves? Nor can we, as Dilthey thought, avoid raising the question with regard to the natural sciences. How far in this case do the objects force an interpretation upon us, how far is it due to our available language and culture?

On these matters the German tradition seems to have diverged from both the English and the American. The English tradition has been in terms of the logic of different kinds of language-games, e.g. the religious language-game. The American tradition, deriving from the original work of Peirce, has concentrated on the nature of signs of many sorts, in relation to behaviour (semiotics), while the German has been more concerned with the nonlogical (e.g.; cultural and emotional) factors in interpretation, and its relevance to man's position in the world. This has been chiefly developed by H. G. Gadamer, a pupil of Heidegger's.

9

From Essentialism to Existentialism: Husserl, the Gestaltists and Heidegger

The word 'existentialism' has certainly reached Britain, though the philosophers commonly labelled 'existentialists' have not aroused much interest here, except in theological circles. *Sören Kierkegaard* (1813–55), a Danish clergyman who wrote a good many unsystematic works in Danish, and did not attract much attention until long after his death, undoubtedly first employed the word *Existenz* in a special religious sense. But he was a bit of a poseur and essentially a theologian, appealing throughout to the overriding truth of particular religious texts. I do not think he was important as a philosopher, or as important for the origination of either German or French existentialism as is commonly supposed.* (The word was perhaps originated by F. H. Heinemann.) The movement was a natural outgrowth of the German tradition of anthropocentrism, of concern for the person as a whole and as active. Hegel, accused of panlogicism by Kierkegaard, was not so far from the centre of this tradition as is commonly believed.

German (and French) existentialism derived partly from Nietzsche but above all from *Edmund Husserl* (1859–1938), a Czech

---

* But others, e.g. George Steiner, take a very different view of him, based largely on his untranslated early work in Danish.

who was active for most of his life in German Freiburg and originally called his ideas 'phenomenological philosophy' (this later,
but inconveniently shortened to 'phenomenology', which already
had another sense). His main work, *Ideas*, employs what has been
called a barbed-wire entanglement of special terminology, but his
basic thoughts are simple and important. His slogan 'Back to the
things!' maintained that philosophy, instead of arguing so much
about how we are supposed to derive our knowledge from our
sensations, should endeavour to describe with great care how
things of various sorts, especially percepta, images, persons,
appear – and how they must appear – to us (phenomeno-logy),
e.g. that a book must appear with three only of its sides visible –
although we have discovered that it has more – whereas this cannot
be the case with a diagram. He claims we can find out what we all
directly know about the essential natures of things in the world by
a process he calls 'bracketing off' (*'einklammern'*) personal peculiari-
ties of vision, catchwords of popular science, prejudices of our age,
and so achieve what he calls a 'seeing of essentials' (*'Wesensschau'*).
A good illustration of his method is Sartre's excellent book
L'Imaginaire (which is divided into two parts: *'Le Certain'* and
'Le Probable'). Husserl states that we know (1) a good deal about
necessary relations in consciousness, e.g. about the dependence of
remembering, expecting, valuing, supposing upon perceiving; (2)
about what he calls the 'syntactical properties of objects' – what
can be denumerated, as pebbles, what can be ordered, as colours;
(3) about regions of the world, as e.g. the physical, the animal, the
personal. Much of this shows similarities with what Wittgenstein
was saying from another point of view, on assembling reminders
about what we can meaningfully say: we see it makes no sense to
say 'the same patch is both red and blue' or 'the stove is in pain'.
All the time human beings are intending something intelligible –
a doctrine worked out by the Austrian, Franz Brentano, and
assumed by nearly all German philosophers – and we cannot
experience the totally unintelligible. If the world were a Heraclitean
world – nothing in it to be picked out and identified – 'Goodness
knows what we should say' (H. H. Price). But, says Husserl,
we know that it is not so. He called this 'eidetic knowledge',

'knowledge of essentials', which takes us beyond any particular illusions that you or I as particular individuals may be subject to.

But how do I know what you know? And how do I know that the world won't change, and become unintelligible to human beings as from next January 1st, as Bertrand Russell imagined? The problem of interpersonality and of time and change were to dominate both Husserl's later philosophy and that of the German existentialists. Husserl in his later works, *Cartesian Meditations* and *Crisis of European Sciences*, claimed that we knew about the nature of other persons and their consciousness by seeing ourselves as a series of (in many ways) different persons as we get older. Into the complexities of his later philosophy we cannot follow him. Two of his pupils, Max Scheler and Nicolai Hartmann, wrote important works on ethics, following his general line. Martin Heidegger was his pupil and long shared his general point of view.

In general Husserl follows Kant, only he regards what Kant calls presuppositions of experience as something directly seen to be true by everyone for all time. It is difficult for him and his followers to account for the real independence of individual persons, and for the great changes in cultural outlook which we find.

It may seem strange that a school of thought which might be labelled 'essentialist' – for they emphasized our power of seeing essential characteristics – should give rise to a school of 'existentialists', who asserted almost the opposite. It is not so strange as appears at first sight, and perhaps becomes more intelligible when we consider the work of the *Gestalt* psychologists – usually so referred to in English, although sometimes translated as 'configuration psychologists'. Wertheimer, Köhler and Koffka were experimental psychologists whose work has been in great part incorporated into accepted psychological theory; they were also philosophers advocating a radical change in our ways of thinking about individuality and time. They also, like Husserl, show that we perceive essential structures of the world, but claim to show that this is due to a process of organization that goes on in time. What we call the ordinary common world comes into being out of our individual private sensations, in the same sort of way as Mickey Mouse comes into being out of the still pictures of the cinema film – an analogy they were fond of employing. The common world they call 'the geographical world', for in it every thing and person has its definite place; but each individual has a private 'behavioural world' – he may for instance cry out at seeing Mickey Mouse; for without question he does *see* him. The behavioural world must be generated out of the geographical worlds by natural forces of organization, of which these authors found many instances. We regularly perceive the world in ways which are not at all what physical science would lead us to expect; some of these are:

Perception of constancies, things as *constant* in size, brightness, colour, when we move about or the light changes;

Perception of relative position and size, rather than absolute position;

Perception of what we live with as 'figures' upon a 'ground' of which there are many curious variations;

Perception of the meaningful qualities of speech and gesture;

Failure to 'organize', in the perception of psychotics, e.g. in Rorschach tests;

The effect upon our perception of having a 'task';

The effect on our perception of social grouping, 'being one of a couple'.

If the facts shown up by their psychological experiments are genuine – and in the main they are incontestable – they raise far-reaching problems of philosophical interpretation (many were raised in another form by Wittgenstein). For Köhler maintains that at least they imply the existence of organizational forces in our brain corresponding to those of which we are conscious (principle of isomorphism); and that this is but one instance of forces tending to organization and disorganization in nature, such as 'entropy' and 'polarity'. So the facts always include a real process going on. It is all very well to say 'back to the things!' but the things are so various: not only sticks and stones, but plants, pictures, clouds, rainbows, noises, words, waves, ghosts. Moreover, a fog is all the time becoming a thing and then ceasing to be a thing. It is a matter of boundedness and constancy. The crucial case for the Gestaltist however is what we may call universal and irremediable illusions, as in the cinema picture or even the press-photograph, which we know is just a series of dots, in the geographical environment.

All this leads the Gestaltist to postulate an individual, human meaningful world, and another common world underlying it, not too dissimilar, related to it through the causal action of the real things upon our bodies.

There is obviously a great deal to be said about this conception of organizational forces, as giving us an account of a sufficiently-common world with sufficiently-individual differences. (It has been well dealt with by the French philosopher, Merleau-Ponty.) It implies, like Freud's model, that each Ego too is a structure of forces, tending however – Köhler thinks – towards certain relatively stable states of dynamic equilibrium. The Gestaltists seem to view human cooperation as that of a collection of machines which have been programmed similarly, but not entirely alike: when they are subjected to the same input of physical forces, they all give the impression of talking about and behaving towards the same things, although what each behaves towards is somewhat different. But the point on which all the Gestaltists agree is that it is a process in time. It is over this, I think, that the Existentialists, notably Heidegger, come to differ from Husserl; we cannot 'see' essential structures in the world, for '*es weltet*' (lit. 'it is worlding') all the time. The one thing we really know for certain and directly is that the world is in a state of perpetual change. How then can we know, or do, anything about it? This is the subject of Heidegger's *Being and Time*, vol. I (he never published a second volume).

Martin Heidegger (1889–   ), a small farmer by origin, took over and discusses in his major work Husserl's conception of philosophy as a description of 'that which manifests itself'.[1] A feature of his (as of Sartre's) philosophy is rejection of all talk about transcendent beings in principle unknowable to man. Like Wittgenstein, he claims that philosophy is only an uncovering of what we all really know, but which is concealed from us through 'the chatter of the common man' (*das Gerede des Man*, where the neuter '*das Man*' = the anonymous '*l'on*'). He has no respect for ordinary language. There is no being which is strictly transcendent; but because of the crucial fact of time and change, all human experience is trans-phenomenal – nothing is known except through an infinity of aspects, everything is the totality of all its temporal aspects.

The criticism made by most English philosophers of the Existentialists is that what they tell us is not philosophy at all but a sort of capricious *a priori* psychology. It is certainly, as is nearly all German philosophy, anthropocentric, believing that we must start from man's position in the world – neither from consciousness, nor from common-sense, nor from the commonly accepted findings of science. But as to how we go on from there, Heidegger (and Sartre) differ greatly from, e.g. Jaspers and others. Traditional philosophy was supposed to tell us about 'all that there is'; claimed to be 'ontology', science of what there is; but Heidegger argues that this was due to the mere prejudice of the Greeks that τὸ ὄν, 'real being', must be immutable, whereas there is nothing that is not subject to change. The science of '*what shows itself*', phenomenology, is the science of the being of beings, *is* ontology – such is Heidegger's lative view. But everything shows itself in time. If every person has a somewhat unique view of the world; if all his behaviour includes a certain creative factor of freedom; if we are not portions of a universal consciousness – how then can we think of there being any certain inter-personal knowledge?

Heidegger's approach is to consider the being of man, and other beings in reaction to the being of man. Man is essentially a being-here-and-now (*Dasein* – not easy to translate) and essentially a being-in-a-world; and that he has some understanding of being is an essential property of his being and of the world which is open to him ('*Seinsverständnis ist eine Seinsbestimmtheit des Daseins*'). We just see two things about man, that he is in an essential relation with a world of objects, which relation Heidegger calls 'caring for . . .' or 'being concerned for' (*sorgen* and its numerous derivatives); and that he essentially understands this world, or as Heidegger says, 'the world is essentially open to him'. When unsophisticated by popular science, we see too that this personal being is but one kind of region of being, and that a person 'stands out (*ek-sistet*) in the openness of being' as something to which the world is manifested.

I venture, hesitantly, to paraphrase: man knows he is only one kind of being among others; that his nature is to act within a world of things and other persons, without which he would not be; and that his nature is to act into time – to 'bestride time' as Heidegger says. And he is integral to the world, for 'world' is a correlative of his being-here-and-now, in one sense at least an environment in which all that is (*das Zeug*) is meaningful for persons: 'Space is in a world, not a world in space.'[2] The world conceived as a mere indefinite aggregate, which happens to include me, is an artificial construct, thinks Heidegger, which apart from popular science we should never hit upon. (The word 'world' however does have an ambiguity about it, which Sartre discusses by means of the old Greek conceptions of τὸ ὅλον and τὸ πᾶν, the whole and the all.) It seems true that we know (1) we are in contact with an indefinite margin of world in all our perception and action (about which the Gestaltists have much to say; and (2) that there is a totality of regularities tied to what we perceive at the moment, so that; e.g. after only a few notes we say, I am listening to Beethoven's Sixth Symphony. 'The world' is not just all that is – what the Chinese called 'the 10,000 things'; they are 'in' the world. But are they? This is to ignore time. Heidegger: 'The world is neither presented [like an object] nor available [like an instrument or piece of furniture], it is all the time coming to be in temporality' ('*Die Welt ist weder vorhanden, noch zuhanden, sondern zeitigt sich in der Zeitlichkeit*').[3] When I wake up, I see it 'worlding' and know that it has been 'worlding' all the time (*Vom Wesen des Grundes*).

In the face of the great problems of 'post-Nietzschean philosophy' (Heidegger), plurality of active persons and real change, Heidegger in the last resort claims we just see that there are various kinds of being and that being is in principle open to man. Man is indeed fallen (*verfallen*), reduced to being the anonymous observer of science (*das Man*); but once philosophy frees him from delusion, there will be inter-personal agreement about what is real, for that is waiting to be uncovered by our speech. Things can be known as they now are, if we have a will to discard prejudices, but because we are individual and temporal beings, because of our freedom, not everything can be known by everyone nor at all times. Mathematical judgements are timeless, scientific judgements are not omnitemporal; all we know is that they hold for a certain epoch. From history we can learn certain possibilities of existence, which can shape our anticipations – what he calls our 'unlocking' of the future. We know directly and for certain something about the process as such – for instance, that there are always persons in a world, beings along with other personal beings; that we shall die and others be born; the general features of time, space, thinghood and personal action. This knowledge is not the result of inductive reasoning, but a necessary basis from which our inductive reasoning about nature must start.

So much for the Heidegger of the first and only volume of *Being and Time* (1927). From two short articles or pamphlets on the nature of metaphysics, commentaries on Plato and Kant, and on poets, especially on Hölderlin, it is not easy to summarize the character of his later philosophy. It can fairly be viewed as an attempt to counter the objection that his work is just anthropology – description of man – but not philosophy, certainly not the whole of philosophy. This objection applies perhaps to Sartre, but certainly not to Heidegger, who is essentially a metaphysician, though rejecting deductive metaphysics of the Aquinas type, not as untrue, but as inappropriate to our epoch. He agrees that philosophy should be about 'being *qua* being'. But this concept is ambiguous, and on this ambiguity Heidegger's later philosophy turns. It is disputable whether this later philosophy is entirely compatible with *Being and Time*.

For, he says, traditional metaphysics has been concerned with beings, *Seiende*, ὄντα, their genera and species, and again, the manner in which different beings, say, stones, cats, persons, spirits, God, are. But now he asks, what is the being of all beings, such that it manifests itself in all these manifold ways? It is not a formless Heraclitean flux, nor do we *make* it intelligible, as Nietzsche affirmed; we find it to be in great measure intelligible. Yet it is a flux, and we know that it appears differently to different persons. So we should not say, 'there are identifiable things' (*es gibt Wesen*) but, 'there is a coming-to-be of things' (*es west*). The being of things, he says, is truth, that which manifests itself, *Unverborgenheit*, ᾽χληθέια. Being is therefore unthinkable without creatures to which it could be manifested, men or men-like creatures who can perceive, imagine, describe and depict. But how far it is manifested does not wholly – though it does partially – depend on us. Some aspects may be hidden from our present epoch. Moreover, understanding of the truth is not altogether a matter of effort, but of mood or 'being in tune' (*Stimmung*). There is every reason for us to think there were beings in the world before man emerged, but we know or conjecture about them only through what is now manifest to us, whereas many aspects of their being may be hidden.

By this sort of language Heidegger strives to do justice both to the meaningfulness and the enigmatic character of things, both to the interpersonal character of knowledge and to the differences of cultures – at the cost of sacrificing all alleged omnitemporal truths and eternally valid laws of nature. All truths are true for an epoch at most, some are highly personal. Philosophy can only interpret being for our historical epoch; there is no more than a certain family likeness between the philosophies of different epochs. For in each epoch what needs to be said is different, and our capacity for 'speaking the being of beings' differs also. In this, philosophy is like art, and like law. In my own words (not Heidegger's): we know there is evolutionary change, and that this brings forth new concepts such as 'atom', 'gene', 'organism', 'society', by which it is interpreted, and again and again re-interpreted. Philosophy is a seeking of language of the highest generality, to enable being to manifest itself as well as may be in this epoch of ours. It must of course go hand-in-hand with experience and experiment of all kinds, but to find suitable words to manifest the character of the process is the special art which is philosophy.

Whence the later Heidegger's obsession with words and etymologies, for which he is jeered at by the English linguistic philosophers. It does seem, as one excellent critic observes, that in his later years he had exhausted what he had laid upon him to say; he is now a very old man. His often unnecessary jargon has led to extreme efforts to interpret what he could have meant in his later works, rather than to decide whether it is true or important. But *Being and Time* is a notable work, and not unduly full of jargon.

10

Jaspers

Karl Jaspers (1883–1969) presents a great contrast to his rival existentialist Heidegger. Less influential in the universities, he seems to have been very popular in Germany, to judge by the 900,000 copies of his works sold in the German language alone by 1963, his eightieth birthday, and their translation into sixteen languages. And yet his style is very far from what we should regard as popular; I should call it good, clear but very leisurely, very professorial German. His biggest systematic works are untranslated. He has written an immense amount, so that to give a fair account of his ideas is trying to put a large gallon into a pint pot.

As a preliminary, something must be said about the man, as his life is by no means irrelevant to his work. A North German, born 1883 of a professional family in the rather remote province of Oldenburg, he trained as a medical doctor, and at the age of twenty-eight was offered the post of medical superintendent of a large mental hospital. But he was warned by the doctors that his health would not stand up to it (he had been told that he could not in any case expect to live beyond the age of thirty). So he turned to theory rather than practice, and became Professor of Philosophy at Heidelberg in 1921. By the age of twenty-eight he had already published a considerable work, *General Psychopathology*, which according to the distinguished writer of the preface to the 1962 English edition is still considered useful as a textbook of the subject.

Jaspers's medical training had a decisive influence on the character of his philosophy. Two other influences may be noted. One was his intimacy with Max Weber, a great personality and many-sided man, who might without exaggeration be called the founder of the modern theory of social science. Central for Max Weber were the problems: what in social and historical enquiry is strictly factual? what is rational estimation of probabilities? what is the factor of personal decision? The other, but negative, influence was his acquaintance with Husserl, who claimed to have established philosophy as a 'strict science' (*reine Wissenschaft*). These two influences led the young Jaspers to

> the two presuppositions that have guided my life: that scientific knowledge is indispensable, without it there is no veracity; but that it has limits, it cannot understand why it itself exists. It leads on to another type of thinking, not compelling by scientific standards, which is philosophical thinking; this illuminates the sources which give meaning to science itself. ... To say the world is matter, in which life, consciousness and thought are included – these are empty words concealing the real gaps.[1]

Some remarks of his on the medical art are illuminating for the motive behind his philosophy. (1) The doctor, he says, can treat the sick body as a mechanism to be got into order again; this is a strictly technical problem (spare-part surgery, chemical treatment) on which some strictly scientific knowledge is available. (2) He can also treat it as a living organism which within limits moulds and regulates its own mechanism. This requires a different attitude – stimulating, relaxing, in a word 'nursing' (as every gardener knows); the medical man has some real empirical knowledge here, but it is not theoretically-based science. (3) He can treat the person as a rational being – he must do so if he needs his cooperation, telling him, e.g., the purpose of the treatment, the probability of cure; this is what Jaspers calls treating him as a 'mere consciousness'. However he is not a mere consciousness, but a creature with fears and hopes and a social position, so that what the doctor decides to tell him will usually affect his body. (4) So the doctor tries to treat the whole man as an object to be cured – a 'case' – telling him what he thinks will be most useful for this, perhaps using suggestive tricks and shock tactics; but such methods often fail, for man is not just a case, and such methods may preclude the discovery of his personal scale of values, 'what makes him tick'. (5) So he may try in the last resort to communicate with the patient 'as one free existent with another free existent', to take on himself the fate of the sick man. But then he must realize that he is neither a technician nor a saviour, that such existential communication is possible for him only with some patients and not others, that the patient may instead treat him, that the illness may serve a deep purpose in the other's scheme of life. On this level the doctor can only risk suggestions.*

I relate this at some length, as it introduces us to Jasper's fundamental conception of different levels of life, with their appropriate types of knowledge, of belief and their rather mysterious interconnections. Jaspers argues that the good doctor operates on all these levels. And the level of responding freedom – what he calls 'existence' – cannot be ignored. In a sense it is a key to the rest.

Another way in which one may seek to exhibit his thought is to relate it to the European philosophical tradition. In his very original history of philosophy – which starts off with Confucius, Socrates, Buddha and Jesus – he names the three seminal philosophers of our culture as Plato, Augustine and Kant. But he is before all else a Kantian, in that he thinks it evident that there is a human element in all our knowledge of the world – it is a world of phenomena – and also that our experience of ourselves as free agents is real and irreducible. Kant with his 'regulative ideas', his 'postulates of practical reason', his 'canons of reflection', began to suggest how we might see these facts together. Jaspers tries to go beyond Kant, but finds the web of reality more complex than Kant did. He holds that we must recognize several different levels of experience, the data of which cannot be rendered in the same language except by using concepts such as 'energy' or 'action'

* The above is derived from an 'off-print' not now available to me, presented by Professor Jaspers.

equivocally and confusingly. Are we each a collection of elementary particles? It is literally nonsense to say that elementary particles choose or act!

Jaspers's central idea, in my words not his, is that freedom of the will is real and important, and is incompatible with an entirely commonsense-realist view of the world. This is a problem that can be clarified, but not given a strictly logical solution, for that would involve treating the agent as an object. It can only be lived with, and the various forms of speculative philosophy are ways of living with it (of course Hume's famous recipe of 'carelessness and inattention' is one way of living with it; but it is not satisfactory for everyone).

The Comprehending and its Modes

Unlike most British philosophers, Jaspers admits the propriety of the concept of 'the transcendent'.* 'It is not knowable that everything is knowable. It is thinkable that there is that which is unthinkable.' We encounter a transcendent cause first in ourselves as agents, in acting and in learning, as an unconditional requirement which is in principle not resoluble into physical, psychical and social cause; then reflecting we see 'boundaries', 'gaps', 'horizons' (he uses all these words) in the world which lead us to think of a transcendent causal factor in things. Such boundaries or gaps are: between physical change and sentience; between sentience and perceiving; between observation of a person's body and understanding his intentions; between mere change and 'history' (a process which implies some directing values); between limited physical systems and the physical universe as a whole. At all these boundaries (what Toulmin calls 'type-jumps'[2]) we are aware of radical novelty which we cannot easily explain in terms available to us. The task of philosophy is above all else to deal with such gaps.

There is a real enigma about the origin of the physical world or the emergence of a human person. It is not just like the riddle of the

* Cf. Kant on 'boundaries' (*Grenzen*) and 'limits' (*Schranken*) in the *Prolegomena*.

grains and the heap, where it is a mere matter of convention at what point we shall say: 'Now there is a heap.' Can we suppose that our manner of speaking literally *makes* the world? We cannot. These are, says Jaspers, 'riddles that we all live with and ignore'. But 'it should effect a transformation in us when once we realize the groundlessness of the world, the unintelligibility of our origin, the uniqueness of man as eye and speech of an otherwise dark and dumb world.'[3]

The starting point for Jaspers is the boundaries I come up against when I reflect upon the use of 'I'. For an 'I-saying-being' goes beyond observation. I see for example that I am not my body; that I am not what I am for others; that I am not my achievements; that 'my past is my mirror, but I am not my past.' I know myself in all these images, by perception and memory. But there is something in me that objects to regarding myself as simply given. That I am this sort of person is something I can actually feel guilty for, even if I do not see anything I can do about it. I have an indirect knowledge about myself (*um mich*) which is not knowledge *of* myself but source of philosophical illumination as to what it means to be an 'I'. Thinking about myself is not 'having ideas' but an 'inner activity', which does not produce verifiable conclusions, but yet is effective.

There is also a second boundary, when I reflect about communication with my fellows. From the phenomenon of a body emitting sounds we can never reach the notion of true language – a sign-system enabling two persons to communicate about what is not present to the senses of either. What then? Let us assume, with Wittgenstein and Whorf, that man is essentially social, and language a form of social life, perhaps innate (Chomsky). We readily see that some forms of language are only intelligible in some forms of society, and there is indeed much of interest to be discovered here (sociological study of language). I must indeed have learned a certain common social language. But I am aware of employing it as my tool, even of wresting it to say what I judge needs to be said. Reflection on language as sociological leads one to recognize 'communication' as existential, to recognize the other X as a free source of truthful speech, as I claim to be. For with a being indifferent to truth, who spoke true or false at random, no communication would be possible.

Reflection on these boundaries make one recognize man as both object and creator of science; product and creator of language, product and creator of history. As a being who is sometimes guided by the mere sense of what is right, man is an 'existent' (Jaspers borrows the term from Kierkegaard), not just an item in the world. And yet he is also an item in the world.

We can try to say a little more about the complexity of this relationship between man and his world.

Life, Science and History

Jaspers, going beyond Kant, says that we have three conflicting views of the world of phenomena. Wittgenstein said we have many different language-games, e.g. the scientific and the common-sense language-games. Jaspers claims that these languages are irreconcilable, corresponding to three different attitudes we take.

First, there is what English philosophers might call the common-sense view, which Jaspers calls the view of '*Dasein*' (lit. being-here-and-now) of a living creature with given practical needs, of which he is partly aware, immersed in the struggle for life. Such a creature sees the world in practical terms. His needs for food, sleep, and in a different way sex, are inescapable, and the conflict they give rise to inevitable. Governed by his needs, he sees it as a world of men, women, plants, animals, houses and tools and uses a corresponding language.

Second over against this is the quite different view we take when doing science. We try to view the world in terms which, abstracting from our needs and our individuality, shall have objective validity for anyone anywhere – e.g. in terms of substances, particles, radiation. This view he terms the view of '*Bewusstsein-überhaupt*' – 'mere consciousness' or 'generalized consciousness'.

There is a third view which we take when thinking about society, its history and institutions. Adopting a term of Hegel's, Jaspers calls this the view of *Geist* (lit. 'spirit'). By spirit, he means man as imagining and making social products such as art and language.

I can only call this the view of historical consciousness. From this point of view we see ourselves as creatures at a certain point in the stream of history, our science for example as just the product of twentieth-century Euro-American man, destined to be superseded, as all previous views of the world have been superseded; for it is just the product of certain historically-developed techniques, certain social institutions, a certain language and so on. In our day perhaps, social determinism is as much a menace as scientific determinism.

For Jaspers, each of these ways of looking at the world is indis-pensable – and incompatible with the other two. To do science we must put out of action what we know about history and about practical life. For instance, we may not say that the conclusions of the scientist are to be explained in terms of his sex drives (*pace* Freud) or of his social-historical position (*pace* Marx). Equally, the requirements of practical living and of social ordering forbid us to view the world in the terms adopted by the scientist. We must realize that we are at once living creatures, historical creatures, scientists – and also 'existents', not only in the world but in a measure moulding it by free activity, a 'cutting-edge' of our soc-iety. And we see that there are subtle connections in all this, for free existence is manifest in different degrees in these three aspects of the life of man.

Now reflection on this network of 'fundamental relationships' (*'Gewebe der Grundbezuge'*) led Jaspers to his quite peculiar con-cept of 'the comprehending'. Is this new term just an asylum of ignorance? It only has point in relation to what he says about 'the modes' of the comprehending, which in his chief work, *On Truth*, he seeks to elucidate by a diagram. He sets at the two poles of his diagram 'the existent' and 'the transcendent', with 'world' in between. 'The world' is the field of various different lines of cogni-tion and action. We might say that Jaspers views life fundament-ally as a dialogue between man and something else, which is manifest in both nature and society, but not reducible to terms of either natural or social causation. We can, indeed we must, think of 'that-which-comprehends', knower and known, agent and environment – to use the term 'world' for the all-inclusive is subtly misleading, for 'world' suggests totality of objects. But all this is only a programme for philosophy to work upon.

Knowledge, Belief and Truth

The scheme he has just suggested is a framework for thinking about our complex relation to the world. Such a scheme seems useful for a time, but not final; it does not have what Jaspers calls 'compelling truth'. It is the result of rational and methodical enquiry, but results only in what he calls 'philosophical belief'. This first part of philosophy he calls methodology – obtaining a well-grounded method of handling the disparate facts of experience. It contrasts with another kind of more speculative belief, which comes from treating certain phenomena as if they had a double meaning, somewhat as a picture is a pattern of colours and also perhaps has a much more esoteric meaning, beyond this simple, first-sight meaning. This is what he calls 'reading the cypher-language of the transcendent, which as it were speaks to us through the world'. For there are features of the world which men have always been inclined to think signify something beyond the merely factual.

This is the field of religion and myth, of what he calls 'serious or concerned art' (*verbindliche Kunst*), of speculative metaphysics. What he calls the 'great cyphers' are the mutual adaptedness of the man and the world, the progress of his science, the infinity of the world and the endlessness of history, natural beauty, physical and moral evil, death.[4] These incite us to attempt imaginative formulations. These also have their legitimate place, and also give rise to a form of philosophical belief or faith. To this I will come back.

Here again one is faced with a translation problem, for German has the one word, *Glaube*, for which we have the two words, 'belief'; referring to content, and 'faith'; referring to an emotional attitude. Jaspers has been criticized for speaking of 'philosophical belief'. Now he does explicitly say that philosophical reflection should give us both insights and a certain attitude of confidence (*Vertrauen*); but he is not to be taken as meaning that philosophy is a sort of religion; indeed he holds that philosophy is always stimulated by and always in tension or struggle with dogmatic religion.

Knowledge and belief in all their different fields seek to formulate truth, which is a special privilege of man by contrast with animals. The task of the philosopher is to move towards truth through all the modes of the comprehending using the criteria appropriate to each. For all important assertion is a discovery, a movement; and all discovery alters the observer in some degree; that is why it involves an element of faith. Knowing is not making, so our claim to speak truth in human language implies that the world is intelligible to man, though we may know it very imperfectly. But truth is only to be found in all the modes of the comprehending taken together, in science, but also in history and in moral and social life.

There are, he says, two main fields of truth, those of 'compelling truth' and of 'historical truth'. This is a source of movement or tension: 'For some people remain within the field of compelling truth [science] in order to evade communication with their fellows.'

Compelling truth comprises: the formally-compelling truths of logic; the axiomatically-compelling truths of mathematics; and the hypothetically-compelling truths of natural science. In these fields there are some universally accepted rules by which propositions can be confirmed or disconfirmed, at least in principle.

By contrast, what Jaspers calls 'historical truth' only claims to be correct at and for a certain time. And that not merely because of new facts, but because of the emergence of new interpretative concepts – e.g. in our time the concepts of 'unconscious', 'information', 'cultures'. So that each age has its own interpretations. (Of course some propositions enunciated by a historian can be strictly scientific and compelling, e.g. Paul could not have written certain epistles, as word-use calculations show. But most go beyond anything that can be called 'compelling'. He points out that Max Weber said of his thesis about the connection of Calvinism and capitalism, only: 'I rate the significance of this factor very high', not 'consider it certain'.)

It is not easy to summarize what Jaspers says about historical truth; I think he uses the term in a wider and in a narrower sense. In the narrower sense, it means that objectivity which the historian and social scientist hopes for and believes in, guided by the ideal of a complete assessment of all the evidence in the light of well-recognized techniques for assessing evidence. This is what Jaspers, following Hegel, calls the ideal of 'spirit'. For this there are available at any time some recognized rules of evidence, philosophical, juristic, etc.

But in a wider sense, all the most important truth is historical because discovered only at a certain time by responsible existents, claiming only to affirm what their personal situation makes evident to them. Luther's 'I can't think otherwise' is the prototype of this kind of truth. In fact of course, as Jaspers points out, there is an intimate tie between the truths which the personal situation of the historian or sociologist reveals to him, and the character of his interpretation, however much he strives for objectivity. There is a connection, yet to claim that his views are completely explicable in terms of his historical or social situation is to saw off the branch on which he is sitting. Important truth is a matter of conscience – scientific, historical, social.

For Jaspers, all important truth 'breaks through' (*durchbricht*) into history at a certain time. Whence it is always the result of struggle, not of detached reasoning. And so for him all non-compelling truth involves the concept of 'authority', a basis of what in my present cultural situation ought to be accepted. He has much of interest to say about different sorts of authority. All authority is based on a claim to superior insight in some field of theory or practice; and so all genuine authority is rooted in the transcendent. He has also much to say about the ways in which authority degenerates and is renewed by 'loving struggle' with the deviant individual (*Ausnahme*), who claims that he also is responding to a transcendent requirement and cannot do otherwise. Characteristic of all the great philosophers is that they have all both had a respect for authority and also been deviants, setting men upon new paths. Where there is a mere chaos of opinions, there is no breakthrough of truth.

I think he includes under historical truth, in this wider sense, correctness both of fact and of value – both new ways of looking at classes of fact, e.g. as evolutionary, and new ways of ordering the life of the individual and of society. For he says that the struggle for truth is a manifestation of practical thought in its four forms which are 'working', 'ordering', 'acting' or 'discovering'. In the end the only criterion of historical truth is a social one – what Jaspers calls 'maximum communication' – widespread recognition that the new propositions are illuminating and fruitful.

For he holds, as against Hegel, that there is no discoverable highroad; 'there is only some tendency for the unity of the comprehending to break through.' One aspect of the process is that which forms the subject of tragedy, on which he has much to say. (This section of his work has been translated.) Tragic failure (*scheitern*) is failure which is nevertheless illuminating, somehow truth-furthering, somehow acceptable. Tragedy is man's greatest endeavour to depict mythically the relation between man and the world-process, but there is also senseless failure in the world, and we must not gloss it over, 'Nature pouring forth without any care her maimed and abortive children', as Hume put it. He concludes: 'We see that there are rifts in being' (*das Sein ist zerrissen*). We can only talk about this mythologically, in pictures none of which is wholly satisfactory.

The Philosopher

The philosopher is concerned, says Jaspers, with the completion of truth. This means in the first place 'orientation in the world', explicating as well as he can the interdependence between different fields of truth – e.g. logical, scientific, legal, economic, moral; this he calls 'exercising the philosophical craft'. But second, he should try to characterize, for his day and age, the unity and discordance (*Zerrissenheit*) that we find in experience. Such is speculative metaphysics. It takes him into the field of the imaginative and the suggestive, the ambiguous meaning Jaspers calls it the 'cypher-language') of things in the world.

For a candid description of man's place in the world is compatible with various possible metaphysical schemes, that of

Spinoza for example, who maintains that all activity is ultimately that of one substance, God; or again that of Leibniz, who holds that individuals are ultimate and that the only comprehending unity is a kind of order – 'God's choice of the best'. To Jaspers, the unity of the comprehending is problematic, and there are rifts. Such metaphysical speculation may also give rise to a kind of philosophical belief. He holds the perhaps paradoxical view that all metaphysical schemes are unsatisfactory, and yet that they are not worthless. For instance no scheme has reconciled 'the secret teleology of living things, the beauty and glory of things' with the hatefulness and senselessness of many features of the world. Jaspers has examined in detail, especially in his latest work, *Philosophical Faith and Revelation*; just where every such scheme falls down. In a sense, we can find a dialectical relation between them, in that if one presses one scheme to its limits – say, the unity of the cosmos or the deficiency view of evil – one is led to recognize the complementary truth of an opposite view. But this does not amount to anything like the Hegelian dialectic; we cannot find a logically-necessary order; 'there is tension [*Kampf*] in the field of the cyphers'. Each appeals to the will and the conscience. I must sometimes act as if all depended on me alone; sometimes as if, however I act, I shall be sustained by a world-order that is greater than I.

But if all metaphysics are inconclusive, why waste one's time with such thoughts – better eat and drink and cultivate our garden? Because Jaspers holds that such thought has a transforming effect (*Umwendung, Umkehr*) on the life of man. Simple positivism also ignores something – the extent of intelligibility, mutual adaptedness and beauty which we do find, and the admiration it arouses. The fact that he feels these questions to be important and is able to think about them, although inconclusively, strengthens his sense of freedom and significance. To think of God as a quasi-person, of a universal natural law, of a possible sense in history as a whole, appeals to man's will, has a liberating effect. Such is his metaphysical view of history, with its two revelatory periods, the axis age and the scientific age. Such schemes might be called programmes for living. They are at variance with one another; all that anyone can say is, 'This is the way I see it at present, but I am ready to learn better.' But such an attitude is more worthy of a free man than, 'What is true? – who cares?' or 'What a lot of odd beliefs there are in the world!' The philosopher must say he does not know, not that he does not care; for such attempts are attempts to capture truth, which beckon yet elude us, in figurative form.

Philosophical meditation, says Jaspers, produces an attitude to life different from that of the unconcerned intellectual or the aesthete; it is akin to the religious. But it utterly rejects the assertion that all truth is incarnate (*leibhaftig*) in certain historical facts of an alleged revelation; this only produces indifference to truth and persecuting fanaticism. And worse, it often exploits men's ignorance in the interests of its dogma – 'You realize how little you know, so anything may be true, so you might just as well accept what we say.' This Jaspers labels 'diabolic'.

What are we to think of this type of philosophy? It is written in a style very unfamiliar to us. It aims at bringing together many different aspects of experience. He deals with subjects such as love and myth, which English philosophers scorn. But he has not given us any explicit treatment of ethics or systematic psychology.

His great contemporary, Sartre, thus characterizes Jaspers's philosophy: 'the cunning attempt of a partially-dechristianized bourgeois to resuscitate the transcendent, wishing to justify his privileges by aristocracy of soul. He is fascinated by an ineffable present, as the result of refusing to look at the future. This sly and soft style of thought is not of much interest.' Sartre regards it primarily as a philosophy which by recommending openness to truth, paralyses action. I think this is unjust. Not everyone is called to political action, as Sartre – perhaps unfortunately – felt himself to be.

For Jaspers, philosophy is rather a preparation for facing adequately what he calls the 'limiting' or 'ultimate' situations of practical life (*'Grenzsituationen'*) – situations in which we know that whatever we decide we can not avoid death, suffering or severe conflict. And yet we know that it is laid upon us, and is possible for us to choose, and in this we know ourselves as free existents, not just social units. But Jaspers regards man's freedom as something intermittent and variable; we are only potential existents.

He sees the exercise of the philosophical craft as an *askesis*, or training for life, rather than a therapy for a disease, as Wittgenstein did. He concludes his principal work, *On Truth*: 'Philosophy arouses, makes us take notice, carries us a little way forward, makes us ready and ripe for the extremities of experience.'

Many of Jasper's smaller books have been translated into English (see bibliography) and two of his three major works have been or are being translated. These are:

1. *Philosophie* (three vols); an early version of his whole system.
2. *Von der Wahrheit* (*On Truth*); the revised version of his system, in which he first introduces the concept of *Das Umgreifende* (variously translated as *The Comprehending* (see above), *The Encompassing* (Schilp) or *The Comprehensive* (Mannheim). In this chapter I have normally followed the formulations which he adopts in *Von der Wahrheit*.
3. *Philosophischer Glaube angesichts der Offenbarung* (*Philosophical Faith and Revelation*), his latest big work, contains much of interest.

11

One-Dimensional Man
and the Principle of Hope

The history of the German people has been remarkably different from ours. It has been a sequence of catastrophes and recoveries from a very low level of life. I cannot help thinking of the ancient poem, *Völuspa* or *The Sybil*,[1] surviving in Iceland in the poetic Edda, so graphically depicting the shaking of the world-tree, the baying of the wolf, the surging of the fire, then the rebuilding by a new race of peaceful gods, when I reflect on the aftermath of the Thirty Years War, of the Napoleonic Wars (in Prussia), of the First and Second World Wars. After each of these utter collapses, widespread hunger, a near-breakdown of civilized order, immense efforts at rehabilitation against obstacles inevitable or imposed. This background left its mark on all the German writers of the twenties and again of the fifties, especially writers of Jewish extraction or of communist conviction, for whom the efforts at rebuilding in the twenties contained the seeds of a worse collapse. With the triumph of National Socialism in 1933, many of these intellectuals decided to emigrate. All the writers to be mentioned in this chapter experienced the trials and uncertainties of emigrant bread in a foreign country, and most returned to a scene of devastation in their own. What England and the United

States owe to this emigration of intellectuals of the German tradition is quite incalculable; one day an attempt will have to be made to publish a reckoning.

Husserl, Heidegger and Jaspers were products of the earlier wave of catastrophe and rebuilding; their major works were of the twenties and thirties. The writers we shall now discuss are essentially products of the second wave. It might therefore in any case be expected that the conception of Utopia, the search for a principle of hope, criticism of one-dimensional man as lost in the meshes of mere facts, would be a feature of their philosophy. But this character of their philosophy has also deeper roots in the tradition.

Under the influence of Plato, with his fundamental conception of an eternal soul, possessed of knowledge of timeless truth, but 'buried in the body', European philosophy has been much concerned with the timeless, formalizable truths of mathematics and logic. It has often attempted to adapt what it wanted to say about life, experience, action to conform to a model set by formal logic. Thus Kant professed to derive his categories of experience from the logical 'forms of judgement'; Leibniz develops his picture of the boundless variety of the world from the logical principle 'praedicatum inest subjecto';* Fichte his whole philosophy from the logical truism 'I is I, therefore not – I is not I'; Spinoza his whole philosophy from the principle that there can logically be only one 'substance which is in itself and is conceived through itself'. These attempts at assimilating philosophy to mathematics are wholly unconvincing, and irrelevant to what these philosophers wanted to tell us.

But Greek and medieval philosophy claimed to transcend the realm of mere facts by referring these to timeless forms or standards – thus 'Socrates is a man and so a rational animal'; 'Justice is everyone exercising his own natural capacities.' So the demand of the philosophers discussed in this chapter is that philosophy must transcend mere fact by referring it not to timeless 'forms laid

---

* 'Every predicate [quality or relation] must be in a subject'. Thus, to take his example, when we say 'David was the son of Solomon' we are really saying 'there was paternity in Solomon and there was filiation in David'.

up in heaven' but to historical possibilities as yet unrealized, only imagined. This is what Marcuse in particular calls the requirement of transcendence. But common to all these philosophers is their criticism of positivism, whether logical or other, of the restriction of reason to facts and hitherto-observed laws; they claim that the attitude has both arisen from, and vitiates, our social system. Imagining Utopias is one necessary and proper function of philosophy. Time and change are ineliminable features of life, which philosophy must recognize, and new social situations give rise to new standards and conceptions.

The German philosophers, returning to a despoiled and divided country, freed from a regime they had good cause to hate, were in no mood to work on refinements of logical formulae, but rather concerned to pinpoint what had gone wrong, and what could be hoped for. None of these writers has attained the position of influence of a Heidegger or a Jaspers, but together they represent an important factor in German thought. This common factor has led to their being commonly known together as the Frankfurt School, a title which however can only be used with some discretion, allowing for loose edges. We shall have to confine ourselves to portraying what seems most characteristic of each, rather than attempt comprehensive reviews of their works.

Apart from the attitudes natural to returning emigrants, this movement of thought has several other roots in the philosophical tradition, which it is worth while to explore:

1) First, the distinction made by Marx between the economic base and the ideological superstructure became a worry to the convinced Marxists, reflecting on their recent past. History in the twenties and thirties had certainly not brought forth socialism, and it did not seem like doing so in the fifties. The triumph of Russian arms had brought forth a bureaucratic state capitalism, under which voices such as Havemann's* pleading for a humanistic socialism without dogma were suppressed.

2) Connected with this is the attempt of the non-socialist

* Robert Havemann, East German, winner of every kind of communist distinction, was removed from all positions of influence for his book *Dialectic without Dogma*.

sociologists, Max Weber and Karl Mannheim, to put the positive science of sociology on a secure footing, through making a sharp separation of social fact from choice between systems of value. For Max Weber, this choice could, though it need not, be rational in an extended sense. *Karl Mannheim* (1893–1947) was a German émigré to England, where he wrote his influential book, *Ideology and Utopia* (original German, 1929). He aimed to make both choices and beliefs into a subject of positive, purely factual study in his *Sociology of Knowledge*, in which beliefs are to be explained as due to extrinsic causes only.

3) The existentialist doctrine that 'decision' (Jaspers) or 'resolution' (Heidegger) is not positively accountable for, and is inevitably a cause of anxiety – and yet, as manifesting existence, is somehow more real or fundamental than positive knowledge.

4) The understandable rebirth, after years of repression, of Jewish messianism, with its belief in a coming utopia on earth, as the result of a secret purpose of history that can only be guessed.

5) Finally, the prestige and popularity after the war of economic planning – a popularity now somewhat tarnished – and in the USA of the new 'rational' theory of games, based on the work of Neumann and Morgenstern.

All these were motives leading to the prevailing concern with utopias, with a 'dialectic of reason', in so far as it concerns itself with the future and is not a merely technical instrument. I shall attempt to discuss three examples of this movement: Ernst Bloch; the 'Frankfurter' in the stricter sense of the term; and Herbert Marcuse.

For all these writers Marx's 'communism' provides the model of a utopia, with the status and meaning of which philosophy needs to be concerned; and they are all agreed that post-Stalinist Russia is in no sense on the way to it.

For *Ernst Bloch* (1885–) communism remains the name of the utopia which philosophy assures us will eventually be realized, through what may be called the mystical character which he attributes to matter. Matter becomes for him, as critics have pointed out, something like the 'world-soul' of ancient philosophy. Born in Ludwigshafen in 1885, he spent the First World War as a pacifist in Switzerland, and wrote there his first major work *Geist der Utopie* (*The Spirit of Utopia*), based on a review of Chassidic and Christian mystical conceptions. Much of this is taken into his later, big work, *Prinzip der Hoffnung* (*Principle of Hope*). The complete edition of this was published only in 1961, and has a curious history. At the time of the publication in East Germany of the first two volumes, Bloch enjoyed as Professor of Philosophy in Leipzig the position of leading philosopher of the German Marxist world. Increasingly suspect as a heretic by the communist party, which declared that mystical philosophy of hope is quite incompatible with Marxism, he remained in the West, where he happened to be at the time of the building of the Berlin Wall; and when his final volume was published in the West the communists felt obliged to follow suit and publish it in the East.

It is a strange work, written in Heideggerian style, taking great liberties with the German language, for me unreadable as a whole. But he has put forward his main ideas in minor works also. For him, man, if the principle of hope is vigorous in him, responds to the urges of nature, primarily of 'hunger', in a way that leads him on beyond his material wants to demand higher forms of social life, in which slavery to work will be abolished and a golden age realized; about this man can only think in symbols. The only necessity is for man to find his place at the 'front' at which history is moving forward to its goal – which is not one of more and more sophisticated technology. All that can be said about it is that it is a realm of freedom, realized not by a God but by the vast un-dreamed-of potentialities of matter – an idea deriving from Engels rather than Marx.

Bloch is evidently a heretic from the viewpoint of orthodox Marxism, since the realization of socialism, then of communism, is not due to economic laws and the relations of production, but to the mysterious evolution of matter. I cannot regard him as a great philosopher, but he represents a line which a disgruntled, quasi-religious, enthusiastic communism might take.

The Frankfurt School, sometimes called the Hegelo–Marxists, were originally grouped round an Institute for Social Investigation in Frankfurt. After the advent of Hitler all emigrated to

America, returning to Germany after the war. The oldest of the group, *Max Horkheimer* (1895–   ), was already a Professor in Frankfurt in 1930, and emigrated in 1933 to New York. Unlike Bloch, he writes good, clear, straightforward German. He collaborated in the USA in *Dialektik der Aufklärung* (*Dialectic of Enlightenment*) with *Theodor Adorno* (originally named Wiesengrund) (1903–59), another leading member of the group. The latter emigrated to Princeton and Berkeley, but returned in 1950 to be Professor at Frankfurt. He was originally a music critic and composer rather than a professional philosopher.* The youngest and I should say most gifted member of the School is *Jürgen Habermas* (1929–   ), who emigrated to the USA, but returned early and has been a Professor in Frankfurt since 1964.

Their work can perhaps best be characterized as sustained criticism of the concept of reason from a Hegelian–Marxian point of view. Horkheimer in his *Eclipse of Reason*, published in the USA in 1947 (*Kritik der instrumentellen Vernunft* in the much enlarged German edition of 1967), claims that the apparent irrationality of the world in which he was writing, with its total war, civil strife, poverty amid wealth, was due to the fact that since the end of the Middle Ages reason had come to be regarded as a mere instrument of the individual subject, something to be applied for his purpose, not something superindividual to be respected. The idea that nature is to be subjected to our use leads really to the subjection of the human spirit. There has been first a rise then a decline of individuality. The idea that concepts such as justice or loyalty should order society became lost, in spite of Hegel's attempt to revive belief in the efficacy of reason through his conception of 'objective spirit'. In *Dialektik der Aufklärung*, a rather odd book, Horkheimer and Adorno sought to show that the quest for 'enlightenment', the overthrow of everything traditional and the admission only of positively testable knowledge as rational overreached itself. So that what was the place of reason as normative in society has been taken more and more by myths, in

---

* His *geistesgeschichtlich* interpretations of musical history greatly influenced Thomas Mann's great post-war novel, *Doktor Faustus*.

particular by the myths of the successful economic man and the sexually emancipated woman.

Adorno calls his remedy 'negative dialectic', propagated in his not very readable work of the same name. This emphasizes the two sides or aspects of Hegel's dialectic: on the one hand man must again become conscious that 'every bit of knowledge is a bodily feeling', that real bodily want is the driving-force in knowing – 'Hegel should have spoken not of the "moment of particularity", but of the particular situation of a particular body' as indispensable to thought, making our thought dependent on our social situation. But on the other hand, to save us from getting immersed in mere fact, the intelligible is always needed as a negative limit; metaphysics must save us from being overwhelmed in the totality of the positive, of mere fact.

In contrast with the orthodox Marxists and Bloch, Adorno maintains that history by itself does nothing. What Marx called 'ideology', rational hope, is essential for the accomplishment of any worth while change. In contrast to Marcuse, Horkheimer hesitates to recommend political activism.[2]

In his principal works,[3] Jürgen Habermas starts from the view that it is philosophical criticism which has imposed an actual limit upon rational behaviour. He builds upon it his criticism of scientificized civilization (*verwissenschaftlichte Zivilization*). Not merely are we so enmeshed in a net of scientific technology that we cannot see how the individual can influence its development in any way, for good or ill; the trouble goes deeper. The reign of positive science has impressed on men the idea that unless there is obviously a scientific answer to a question, the question cannot or should not be asked – there can be no answer. Thus being rational has come to mean restricting one's reflections to what is technically possible and the discrediting of all reflection on life as a whole – the discrediting of all discussion upon interest, inclination, hope, individual identity. This again leads to 'decisionism', the view that either a decision is determined by definite scientific facts or it must be a matter of spinning a coin, and finally to the belief that after sufficient collection of facts the solution of all conflicts can be finally computerized in a cybernetically-governed society. This is 'a bad Utopia, a dominance of absolute technical power over history'.

In his later work, *Erkenntnis und Interesse*, Habermas follows up Kant's conception, in the latter part of the *Grundlegung*, that practical reason has an interest in discovering the truth (which Kant calls a '*pure* interest') apart from the interests it has in gaining particular satisfactions. Besides positive science and technical reasoning, philosophy is needed as '*Selbstreflexion*' – to keep asking ourselves where we are getting to, with the aim of freeing ourselves from self-deceptions and finding better interpretations and modes of communication with our fellows. Here Freud's psychoanalysis can provide a model, for, as we saw, his work was essentially one of finding new interpretations of people's speech and actions. Habermas however claims that this model can be, and should be, applied to society as a whole. What in the individual is self-reflection is in a society self-education. Such reflection upon its experience is just as important for the self-maintenance of a particular society in the struggle for life as is physical work.

The fault of Marx, according to Habermas, was to regard all acquisition of knowledge as 'production'; but society does not consist of classes with fixed ideologies; education – change in ideology, probably accompanied by change in relative power and by change in language – is going on all the time. Freud's basic idea, that owing to the niggardliness of nature a high level of repression of drives of the individual is required for the maintenance of the society, needs to be constantly re-examined, largely on account of the immense development of technical reason, but not re-examined by technical reason. For besides the discipline which really is necessary for the maintenance of the society, there are always specific class and group pressures inducing self-deception, preventing a re-examination that should be truly rational. Society requires philosophy to keep alive the question whether existing repressions are really necessary, and whether new interpretations leading to better communication between different groups of citizens are not possible. Otherwise the change in society will be a mere blind conflict of force. Such philosophy must be motivated by 'a principle of hope', by Nietzsche's, 'See, how much is still possible!'

The man who has gone furthest in claiming that philosophy is 'engaged', requires definite social action, is *Herbert Marcuse* (1898–), no relation to Ludwig Marcuse. He was a close associate of Horkheimer's and emigrated in 1934 to the USA where he became professor at Columbia, Harvard and Brandeis, and has been since 1965 professor in the stormy surroundings of the University of California. He must not however be thought of as just the rabble-rouser which he is sometimes reputed to be; his *One-Dimensional Man*, for example, is a serious philosophical work, written in a clear and vigorous style, and quite properly claiming the attention of the student generation. He has never since his emigration held a teaching post in Germany, but his visiting lectures and works in German have won him a unique position among the New Left in Germany. Perhaps he now belongs rather to the American tradition than to the German; but he cannot be understood except as a product of the German tradition, having been a pupil of Heidegger and having written his first work on Hegel. Here I consider only his major work, *One-Dimensional Man*. Other characteristic works are *Eros and Civilisation*, *Psychoanalysis and Politics* and *Psychologie, Politik and Utopie*.

Developing more forcefully the thesis of the Frankfurt School, Marcuse shows what man has lost through the spirit of positivism or 'scientism', which has permeated every cranny of our society; in his view this is deliberately promoted by the established élites that aim to keep society just as it is. It is a kind of society which appears to be rational, since everyone – apart from groups like the unemployable, the blacks and some immigrants – is apparently so satisfied with his ever-rising standard of living and against any rational action that would disturb the functioning of the sophisticated technical machine that provides this standard of living. Far from being dismayed, as Habermas suggests, at their inability to interfere with it effectively, people do not want to interfere. Yet the machine is not so rational as it appears at first glance; the well-being is won at a high cost. This cost includes the instilling through the mass-media of all kinds of unnecessary wants, requiring even greater accumulation of resources; the exclusion of any meaningful political activity by the ordinary individual citizen; a degradation, through commercialization, of culture, art, the erotic, poetry, indeed of common speech so that the citizen has progressively lost the power of what Marcuse calls 'sublimation' – the means for carrying his imagination beyond the sphere of everyday fact.

In a chapter of biting sarcasm on the 'ordinary language' philosophy of Wittgenstein, Ryle and Austin – certainly unfair to Austin – he shows how philosophy has been similarly degraded to discoursing about 'the broom being in the corner' apart from all the intentions and actions which might make such a sentence meaningful. Society is not a product of chance, but of a whole range of 'projects' conceived by the controlling élites; and man must again become capable of forming counter-projects. The capitalist system is based on repressive tolerance, on having instilled the idea that since almost any behaviour is tolerated, political action is of no importance or efficacy. But counter-projects must be tested by their likelihood of satisfying real human needs, while yet maintaining the productive powers of civilization and furthering a pacification of society; a damping-down of conflicts. The conceiving of such projects will be the work of élite minorities, but the power for realizing them must come from marginal elements in society (e.g. the students, though he does not say so) who are not content with the chance of a higher standard of living which the system offers. Philosophy has a practical task, of regaining its power of transcendence of present facts and propagating hope.

Marcuse goes beyond the rest of the Frankfurt School in making political action a necessary outcome of genuine philosophy. He bases this on an analysis of Freud's theory of instincts or drives. We have seen that Freud believed that all culture, all civilized life, required some repression of instinctual satisfaction – some subordination of the pleasure principle to the reality principle, or, in his later terminology, of Eros to a measure of socially necessary aggression; so that in all moral, social and intellectual freedom there is a measure of unfreedom. Now Marcuse asserts that this is true, but that it is no longer necessary. The culture which the old traditional society achieved by the use of force and censorship, modern society achieves by controlled liberalization, repressive tolerance, so that people's instincts are repressed without them realizing it and without necessity. The authority of the established élite groups has been introjected, internalized so that most people submit willingly to the sacrifice of pleasure. Now Marcuse claims that freedom need be no longer limited by scarcity, so that repression of instincts for the sake of culture is no longer necessary. He demands the end of utopias and the clear distinction between what is absolutely unfeasible through physical and biological law, and that which just happens to seem unfeasible in our own society. His pamphlet 'Liberation' (1969), claims that much can be accomplished by the marginal forces in American society – students, Black Power, etc.

It is indeed likely that every culture goes in for some repressions which are unnecessary, survivals from a situation in which they once were necessary to the self-maintenance of the society. But the doctrine that no repression of instincts is socially necessary may have an appeal precisely to those for whom it is psychologically dangerous. And if it is based on the assertion that man's life is no longer governed by natural scarcity of resources, so that he no longer has any need to struggle for life, a glance round the world as a whole, with ever-growing population pressing upon the food-supply, seems to show that this assumption that we can all sit back and enjoy ourselves without limit is patently nonsensical.

MacIntyre's severe criticism of Marcuse[4] seems to rely upon three points. The first is that his account of modern technological society is untrue – it simply is not so monolithic as he makes out, nor are people so contented with their standard of living as never for a moment to contemplate any resistance to authority. The account may well be, is no doubt, exaggerated; yet when one thinks of the complexity of modern company organization and of governmental organization, and of their intermeshing, there is some truth in this account which is worth bringing out. The second point is Marcuse's depreciation of formal logic in comparison with other modes of reasoning, a point which I shall consider below. The third is that he is an élitist – well, why not? Perhaps an extreme rationalist must logically be élitist.*

Marcuse's account of the place of imagination and reason in choice may have been influential in giving rise to the very typical American creation of the science of futurology, which already has two university departments devoted to it. The conception of 'futurology' was proposed by another German émigré, Ossip P. Flechtheim (1909–), since 1959 Professor of Political Science at the Free University, Berlin; but popularized by the American, D. Thompson, in his book *The Foreseeable Future*. Forecasting does indeed raise deep and fascinating philosophical problems relating to 'the second dimension of our knowledge', as Marcuse called it. For as B. de Jouvenel in his excellent book, *The Art of Conjecture*, points out (1) 'facts' are quite useless for decisions – what is needed is a forecast of what facts there will be; and (2) a forecasting of people's values, their relative weight, and their likely changes is just as essential as a forecasting of likely facts. 'A fan of possible alternatives' can only be derived from a calculation of what is physically possible together with an estimation of what people in various different possible situations are likely to want. This does not imply that we approve the valuations which we forecast. This somewhat pretentious new science does not however seem to have taken root in Germany, and so is outside the scope of this book.

What can be said of this movement in philosophy? Philosophy should indeed make us aware of the variety of cultures and suspicious of the argument that any change whatever is the thin end of the wedge, leading on in unsuspected ways to ultimate social disaster. We need to cultivate 'rational imagination' of what might very well be altered. The young are right to insist on this. Do we need utopias? A utopia is essentially something mythical, involving concepts incompatible with those with which we communicate about our present world. The myths of heaven or hell after death, and salvation by the blood of Christ, the myth of a classless society, the myth of our nation as the best, the myth of an

* Cf. R. Wollheim, 'A Paradox in the Theory of Democracy', in Haslett, *Philosophy, Politics and Society*, vol. 2.

absolute end of struggle or contest – all these are manifestly not true in any ordinary sense, yet powerful agents in the development of longer-term human effort – building cathedrals, creating a health service. Is any kind of quasi-rational discrimination between myths possible, or is each 'in order just as it is'? Perhaps some myths are appropriate to some places and epochs, not to others, e.g., the myth of national superiority to the undeveloped countries, the myth of Christianity for the excessively warlike Vikings, or for the old now, who have insufficient sources of hope otherwise.

Utopias do not necesarily reinforce revolutionary action. Jean Améry (originally Belgian but living and active in Germany) and Helmut Kuhn, a notable Catholic philosopher, have stressed the need to distinguish utopias which we know – either from science or revelation – will be realized whatever we do (such are the Marxist classless society and the Christian reign of Christ at the end of the world) from utopias which can be hoped for. Each of these gives rise to markedly different kinds of reasoning and activity. Thus, Ralf Dahrendorf, sociologist, rector of a new experimental university, European Commissioner, regards concentration upon utopias as an all too conservative factor in life.[5] A utopia, he writes, is essentially a state of things in which no change occurs any more for ever. Whereas historical time is a process in which, along with some likely recurrences predictable by science, absolutely unforeseeable novelty manifests itself. For all we know, History may come to a full stop tomorrow through the explosion of a sufficient number of hydrogen bombs; this seems to be quite possible.

W. H. Auden has recently given a good account of the relation of history to myth or poetry, and of their intermediate forms.[6] What then is a myth? That is a question that has exercised many thinkers and would require a whole book. For our purposes I take myth to be a serious story intended to convey in an imaginative form something of great importance.

There are in principle two different kinds of explanation of social occurrences: in terms of physical and psychological causal laws; and in terms of what people really intend, imagine they intend, or do unintentionally. Neither way of looking at human action can be dispensed with; it is a largely unsolved task of philosophy to show us how to think of them together, perhaps the most important task of our times. We know a good deal about the techniques of scientific discovery; the techniques of unequivocal communication; the techniques for effecting rational social order. Philosophy needs to see these together. As MacIntyre says, formalizable deductive reasoning has always had its place in human communication. Man has always needed to understand 'or', and 'not'. But discovery, communication and social action are nearly all matters of *probable* reasoning, of which there are many distinguishable sorts, some very general, some relating to particular fields, such as medicine or philology (e.g. *difficilior lectio portior* – 'what is harder to understand is more likely to be correct'). And 'stand still or I shoot' certainly does not imply that I shall shoot if you do not, nor that I shall not shoot if you do. Other circumstances may arise, or I may simply change my mind.

If 'futurology' means the thorough discussion of all the different sorts of reasoning, about facts and about values, which we employ when reflecting about, or acting into, the future, it will certainly be of importance. The general thesis of the Frankfurt School is that the scientific view of the world offers only a limited view for limited purposes and that we cannot reduce reason to rules.

The Contribution of the
German Tradition in Philosophy

European Philosophy since Descartes

It is a remarkable fact, as already remarked in the Introduction, that since the break-up of Christendom at the end of the Middle Ages there have only been three important traditions of philosophical thought in Europe – the British, the French and the German.* There have of course been thinkers of other nations whose contributions have been important, such as Giambattista Vico or Sören Kierkegaard. But the philosophy written in English, French and German shows a continuity of traditions, each influencing the other two, but each with a decided character of its own. Nor is this altogether due to the characteristics of the language employed, although the adaptability of German, like Latin, to the use of long paragraphs, or the linear character of English due to its lack of inflections, may have something to do with it. Differences can also be due to the medium employed – the journal read by a fair-sized group of cultivated people, the salon, the lecture hall. Other reasons that have been given, such as the addiction of the

* For the last hundred years there has been a quite distinct American tradition also.

British to common sense and the lack of it among continentals, are much more dubious!

I have suggested that the best way to come by an understanding of these similarities and differences is to enquire into the motivation of the philosopher. In our time philosophy has become a somewhat dubious subject, many such as Reichenbach holding that it can and should be completely replaced by the special sciences; but we do still have departments of philosophy in our universities, and for many continentals it forms a subject in the curriculum of their secondary schools. During the period we have had under review it has given birth to many specialisms which have become major departments in their own right – in one university the professor of natural philosophy is a pure mathematician, the professor of experimental philosophy the senior physicist. There is no complete agreement either with regard to the boundaries, or the proper methods of philosophy. Many methods have been advocated for philosophy, and proved to be passing fashions; such were the claims for dialectic, for a perfect language of rigorously defined symbols, for ordinary language from which technical terms were excluded, for unified science. In a sense, as has been said, every man can be his own philosopher; yet if he wishes to communicate with his fellows on these topics, he is almost obliged to employ the language and methods that have been developed by a tradition, European or Oriental. Within each of these European traditions there is a certain consensus as to which have been great philosophers. There is undoubtedly a certain affinity to be observed between philosophy and the literary arts, as well as with mathematics and science. The exploration of these affinities has been a major subject of the German tradition, and requires further discussion, if we are to understand the European type of philosophy.

The work of the great imaginative poets such as Shakespeare, Goethe or T. S. Eliot is closely akin to that of the philosopher. They reveal to us truths about life and nature that were not obvious to us before. They do this however by means of imaginary characters and situations, in a way that is not open to the philosopher to the same extent. Consistency and comprehensiveness – seeing all round the subject he has chosen – are not unimportant for the literary artist; they are of central importance for the philosopher. The philosopher has to show greater consistency and persistence in teasing out the problems with which he feels himself confronted, especially the clashes between opinions that at first sight seem acceptable, without letting his imagination deflect him from his task. Locke was a philosopher whose work is constantly illuminated by imagination and personal recollection, but these are kept within bounds. A philosopher who has successfully used both genres to illuminate philosophical problems is Jean-Paul Sartre. In the case of Plato and Nietzsche we are never quite sure when their work is to be judged by the standards of philosophy or of poetry.

We can best understand the common trends in European philosophy by looking at the motivation of the philosophers rather than their method. The customary divisions into rationalists, empiricists, idealists, realists, positivists, metaphysicians, have great drawbacks; all these are extremely ambiguous terms, so that every notable philospher could be grouped under more than one. In particular, every philosopher is both a rationalist and an empiricist, and a metaphysician too, in so far as he proposes novel ways of looking at the world which he claims to be fundamental or especially significant.

The first, usually dominant, motive of philosophers, from Socrates – indeed from Xenophanes and Heraclitus – onwards, has been a desire to clarify, in the sense of destroying, baseless opinions, prejudices and superstitions, especially religious and political superstitions, which seem to them to be confusing men's minds and inhibiting their action. This is what the philosophers of the revival in the late seventeenth and the eighteenth centuries called 'enlightenment'.

Some, but only some, of these confusions and superstitions may certainly be due to ambiguities of language – and the clearing-up process may well be called 'analysis', the special feature of British philosophy. The earlier Socratic dialogues consist precisely in this, in asking young men for the definition of a word such as 'piety' or 'friendship' and showing by examples the confusions in which they involve themselves in various situations of life. Philosophy does not go in for experiments, except for 'thought-experiments' which are often valuable – e.g. 'What would we say if we could see and hear what is apparently "a person" in a certain place, but not touch him; or if a mere wish could transport a person to another place?' But it does not follow that analysis is of words and arguments for their own sake; rather it is to help us to diagnose experience rightly, or better. If, following the practice of the acknowledged great philosophers, one defines philosophy as a very persistent attempt to think truthfully about great issues, philosophy cannot ignore trends in the science, art, religion and politics of its time; it must be open to the experiences of its age which seem important. It may be able to make clearer to scientists and political theorists which problems are essentially semantic, connected with the usage of concepts (e.g. of 'simultaneity' or 'gene'), and which are factual; but whether it helps in this way or not, it should help to orient, and so to clarify, the outlook of a certain age. That means that it will be dated, no doubt, though still quite likely to be of interest to other ages. We may not now be interested in Hegel's philosophy of nature, rather in other parts of his system, but it was not an impertinence on his part to write it; nor of Bergson to write *L'Evolution Créatrice*.

One method of analysis much practised by British and some French philosophers, but much less by Germans, has been called 'reductive analysis' – the method of trying to solve complex problems by reducing them to the simplest possible terms. This was recommended as a sovereign method by Descartes, father of European philosophy, in his *Discourse on Method*. Unfortunately it is not always agreed what the simplest terms are. In general, British philosophy has taken them to be simple ideas of sense and simple ideas of reflection (Locke), the smallest units or items of consciousness. This method has not been followed in German philosophy (except perhaps by Herbart); indeed the philosophers called phenomenologists, Gestalt psychologists and existentialists have claimed to show that it is fundamentally mistaken. The quest for the unit of consciousness is a will-o'-the-wisp.

In following the process of enlightenment, it is necessary to observe that the important issues vary from age to age and country to country. Some are cleared up for good, such as the relation between man and the fossils, which so exercised the eighteenth century; some persist in a new form, as for example the problem of man's responsibility, which now presents itself in a mathematical rather than in a theological setting.

The British method of analysis tended until recently (Austin and Hampshire) to assimilate questions about action to questions about the content of consciousness, and elucidate the former in terms of 'feelings of approbation', 'quanta of pleasant and un-pleasant feeling', and 'different kinds of pleasant feeling' (J. S. Mill) and the like. Neither has this line been followed by German philosophy, which has taken it as a simple datum that we under-stand what it is to act – which is not the same as any kind of know-ing – and that we must start not from consciousness but from the embodied person. This is not to say that the Germans were not often spurred on by British and French philosophy, as in the famous case where Kant in the *Prolegomena* tells how Hume woke him from his dogmatic slumbers.

This powerful motive to enlighten runs through the course of German philosophy, a will to educate by destroying baseless beliefs, especially religious beliefs. It is a powerful motive in Kant – with his motto *'sapere aude'* – and Lessing, but also in Hegel, Marx, Schopenhauer, Nietzsche, Freud and Jaspers. The Hegelo–Marxists contend that it has overreached itself and paralysed action. Marx's aspiration, to find a unity of theory and practice, has been a dominant motive in most of his predecessors and successors.

There is another quite different motive, equally strong in all European philosophy, and very marked in German philosophy. It is the motive to achieve completeness and comprehensiveness. This leads to developments in philosophy akin to those which in literature and art are called Romantic.

It seems on the whole inappropriate to talk of 'Romantic philosophy' and yet not wholly inappropriate to speak of 'philo-sophy of the Romantic era'. The term 'Romantic' in the sense of 'fantastic' occurs as early as the seventeenth century; but as a term characterizing a certain kind of literature and art it certainly emerges in Germany first of all, and in the latter part of the eighteenth century. In 1803 we find Jean-Paul writing of the Romanticisms of speculative philosophy. Not until 1819 do we find in England a reference to the Romantic as a principle of literature or art. In France the emergence both of the characteristics of the movement and of the term is certainly later. Diverse features of the Romantic movement are: the cult of the emotions, the cult of individuality – notably of the genius, interest in the hitherto neglected Middle Ages, in the occult, in oriental civilization, in folk-poetry, and in the languages of the less familiar peoples in which it was written, in differences of national culture. In Britain the movement decidedly took its origin in poetry, with *Lyrical Ballads* (1798) (Wordsworth and Coleridge) and the first works of Byron. In Germany it greatly affected both the subject matter and the methods of philosophy. Friedrich Schlegel and Novalis, both around the turn of the century (e.g. Novalis in *Christianity versus Europe*, and Friedrich Schlegel in his 'Speech on Mythology'), expounded the theory of the Romantic movement.

To revert to the acknowledged philosophers, Schelling's work on religion and mythology, Fichte's Ego-philosophy, Hegel's description of such states as 'unhappy consciousness', 'self-alienation', 'spiritual humbug', 'freedom and terror', are concerned with matters hitherto considered to be quite outside the field of philosophy and may be called 'Romantic'. The same is true of Schopenhauer's orientalizing philosophy – on how to kill the will-to-live – and Nietzsche's examination of the forms of self-deception, and his joyous acceptance of the great variety of values to be found in the different great historic cultures. From this movement to extend the purview of philosophy derives what is commonly called 'existentialism' – a 'romantic rationalism'.[1] Romanticism in philosophy is often held to originate in the cult of sensitivity by Rousseau, and in the French Revolution; these both played a part, but not I think a decisive part; such changes of outlook cannot be attributed to a single event, they are in the air, as we say. (Nor is the distinction sometimes made between the pre-Romanticism of 'Storm and Stress' before 1789 and the Romanticism that followed of much significance to explain the change which came over German philosophy around 1800.)

'Solipsistic idealism', the feeling that the whole world is my presentation (Schopenhauer), is a state of mind that was explored by the Romantic philosophers. The uniqueness which they attached to every individual – instead of the common humanity always presumed by their predecessors – perhaps derived from the very origin of German philosophy in Leibniz's 'principle of plenitude', according to which God created as many different individuals as was logically possible, however evil some of these individuals might seem to us; Leibniz had a strong sense of the truly astounding variety of life in the natural world. Existentialism takes over this sense of utterly individual choice, and tends to concern itself with the obscurer states of anxiety, care, love, conversion, which already came into view with Schelling and Schopenhauer. It is a proper concern of philosophy to try to extend its boundaries, especially as the sciences and other organized departments of knowledge extend theirs. This raises the questions with which the Frankfurt School has been concerned.

As I see it, the movement towards Enlightenment and towards Romantic comprehensiveness gives rise around 1850 to a third trend in European philosophy, which is with us still, and which I have called 'sociologism'.

Starting from Descartes' 'What do I really know?', philosophy had been a highly individual quest. This individualism was heightened by the Romantic movement with its concern, sometimes excessive, for originality; whereas mankind is depicted by Hobbes as a collection of men all fundamentally alike and so susceptible of social 'mechanics', and history is regarded by Lessing as 'the education of the human race', of men all fundamentally alike and destined to go through the same stages of development. Herder already recognized the great differences between national cultures. But Hegel viewed the individual as in part the creation of objectified spirit, i.e. of institutions that differed from time to time and place to place; and also as being essentially and inevitably in a certain position in civil society. He also viewed history as a contest between different folk-spirits. This brought a new dimension into philosophy, which I can only term the sociological movement.

Man's thought as well as his action is plainly influenced not only by the natural conditions under which he lives, by climate (Montesquieu) and available forces of production (Marx); it is also influenced by social and historical conditions. We have to find categories, suitable concepts, for thinking about this, if we are to get a true view of our state. The philosophical reaction to Hegel due to Marx and Comte is often labelled 'positivism' or 'realism'. But these words are highly equivocal. Just as in visual art, so in philosophy there are many sorts of realism; as we saw with the Vienna Circle, one sort makes units-of-consciousness ultimate (Titchener, a great exponent of this psychology, recognized some fifty such units); another sort makes the ultimate physical entities, the 'pions', 'baryons', etc., the real units (physicalism). The motive of Enlightenment, with its careful analysis of particular concepts, especially of 'idols of the tribe' (Bacon), should be always with us. But since Hegel and Marx the recognition has grown that the culture of a certain society or a certain historical epoch is to a certain extent a whole, in which science is but one item; consequently the recognition that we need to consider together the economic possibilities, the art, the current moralities of nations and sub-groups has become commonly accepted to a growing extent in England and the USA.[2]

For Marx indeed the only important social formations are classes based upon relations of production – primarily bourgeoisie and proletariat; all science, art, morality is superstructure – not without its interest and importance, but subject to the great overriding laws of history, which are of a socio-economic character. The philosophy of nearly half the world, so far as it is permitted to be published, is based on these presuppositions. But in the West, and within the three great traditions of which we have been speaking, it is generally held that this philosophy of culture and of history is too simple. There are important group-formations beside those resting upon relations of production, and anyhow these relations do not seem to divide men simply into bourgeois (or capitalists) and proletarians. Nor can a serious historian accept the simple Marxist view of base and superstructure, the latter being responsible only for timing and minor variations. There is as much truth in Max Weber's thesis that the protestant ethic produced capitalism, as that capitalism produced the protestant ethic; either thesis alone is too simple. The notion of 'culture', both in the sociological sense as the totality of preferred attitudes and customs of a group which are somehow interconnected (*Kultur*), as well as in the more restricted sense of personal self-development (*Bildung*), has been the subject of much German philosophy, especially that of Herder, Hegel, and Dilthey; there are many problems to do with the rise of cultures and of cultural change which we are far from understanding as yet, for all the sociological research which is going on. There are many kinds of social grouping, not merely economic, but also religious, military, academic, technical, which are sources of a characteristic culture or sub-culture of their own.

Culture, Morality, Language and Religion

Philosophy is evidently an ingredient in some cultures. Whether anything like philosophy will emerge depends on certain features of the culture; like science, philosophy has emerged in very few cultures – less than half a dozen. There is a close kinship between philosophy and natural science, but it does seem possible to have one without the other, for a time at least. Philosophy certainly implies the possibility of *Bildung* – 'self-culture' – which presupposes the existence of some classes or social groups that have leisure. Philosophy may or may not be an ingredient in a particular culture; it seems still to be an ingredient in European culture. The present status of philosophy in Britain is certainly questionable, and I return to this question after an attempt to see what light the German tradition may throw upon the nature and tasks of philosophy.

Our sociological outlook and the new type of history based upon it that emerged around the turn of the century leads us to look upon all manner of human actions and productions as items-in-a-culture, to be explained simply in terms of social relations – in some cases to be correlated with one another mathematically, as for instance in the well known studies correlating religion with sex, age, and economic grouping. Yet this can lead to a very defective view of at least three fields of human activity – language; morality and art – and perhaps religion.

(a) *Language* is indeed an ingredient, perhaps the basic ingredient, in every culture (and sub-culture of smaller groupings). Our thought and our perception are moulded at every turn by what we can say. Anthropologists tell us: 'A certain tribe has words only for "one, two, three, four, five, a few, many"; there is no such thing as "seven birds" in the world of that tribe'. And language is moulded by the social habits and practical activities of the people of that culture; some Amerindian tribes are said to have no word for 'war', others no word for 'peace'. Anyone familiar with more than one language knows how one's thought and observation are influenced by the features of the language – for example, by its possession or non-possession of a definite article (Russian).

Yet language, like morality, and perhaps religion, is not something that is just a brute fact of one's social milieu; it is creative. In the first place it seems to be possible – although often with great difficulty – for any human being to communicate with any other. In the second place, the astounding achievement of a young child in being able to use correctly phrases that it has never heard before points to something like a deep grammatical structure common to all languages and innate – the line of thought of Noam Chomsky. And finally, it seems that language can be continually and deliberately extended by means of artificial devices based on mathematical symbolism. The topic of language has been approached from these different directions, culminating in the work of Wittgenstein, but also of the existentialists, with their emphasis on 'communication', 'authentic' and 'deceptive'.

For there are in every culture different levels of language appropriate to different sorts of communication, and it seems almost certain that every culture has to have myths, and rituals expressing myths, if it is to be durable. This sort of language attempts to portray imaginatively, generally by the use of simile, man's relation to nature and to his fellows, his fears and his aspirations. It seems certain that myths are originally traditional and bound up with ritual. Which comes first, the myth or the ritual enacting it, is a fascinating subject, often leading to arguments like that of the hen and the egg – which we cannot pursue here. Myths and the mythological type of language by means of which men tell imaginative stories about the most serious and critical features of life cannot be created at will by an individual. But personal mythologies can be and are created, by such writers as Plato, Paul, Blake, Goethe, T. S. Eliot, by utilizing material and language drawn from traditional anonymous mythology – such as Atlantis, Faust, Tiresias. Perhaps in time these may grow, like Marx's myth of the Communist utopia; who knows? Perhaps the basic purpose of mythology is to link the necessities of nature and of history with the needs and aspirations of individual man, and so with morality and religion and serious art.

(b) *Morality* is also from one point of view an ingredient in every culture; it can be observed and compared over space and over time. It can be taken to signify a set of approved and disapproved customs relative to sex relations, status relations, exchange relations – what Hegel called *Sittlichkeit*, 'morals-as-fact'. But the aspect of morality which Kant first stressed, 'the morality of conscience' (Troeltsch), personal morality, is not just an item in culture, but a precondition of any culture, creative of culture. Without some sense of unconditional duty – e.g. to keep some promises (Nietzsche) – it is hard to see how any culture could exist. German philosophy since Kant has rightly treated morality as in some sense *sui generis*, not just a social product, but a manifestation of reason operating within the 'parliament of instincts' (Konrad Lorenz).

(c) *Religion* is an extremely equivocal concept, much more so than morality. Among the many religions to which this term has at some time or other been applied there is scarcely anything in common – e.g. between the primitive animism of a New Guinea tribe; original Buddhism or Confucianism; Judaism and Islam. In most contexts it denotes an ingredient in a certain culture, a collection of rites, customs, attitudes, closely bound up with objective morals (*Sittlichkeit*), often the most striking ingredient in the culture, marking off, e.g. Hindu from Muslim. But there is a sense in which religion signifies a personal attitude to the whole of life akin to personal morality; and in this sense it is creative of culture, and very often transformative of culture; e.g. in the cases of Paul or Luther. Like personal mythologies in art and literature, it can only come about by utilizing the conceptions available in the factual religion of the individual's culture; but they can be utilized creatively, as by the great religious reformers.

(d) *Art* again is an equivocal concept. It may signify no more than a delightful play with colours, tones and words – and why not? But some art is in both in intention and in fact revelatory, both utilizes creatively and extends a visual language. As such it is akin to language and akin to religion, not just an item in a culture, but creating and transforming it – as perhaps Michelangelo and Wordsworth may be said to have transformed a culture they found. This being so, Kant was not wrong to treat art as symbolic of morality, nor Schelling and Hegel to treat it along with religion.

The Special Contribution of the German Tradition

Those who in the course of three centuries won recognition as philosophers within and beyond the bounds of the old German (Holy Roman) Reich were on the whole recognized in their own time as outstanding personalities. Leibniz knew the leading intellects of all Europe, and tried hard to conspire with Bossuet to heal its wounds deriving from the religious wars. Kant, without ever moving from his remote native Königsberg, had by the time of his death stirred men's minds throughout the length and breadth of the Empire, while not making the slightest concession to popularity in his manner of writing. The personality of Herder powerfully affected Goethe and the Weimar circle. Fichte, a queer character, stirred the German nation with his *Speeches*. Hegel, again without the slightest concession to popularity, divided most educated Germans into either enthusiastic followers or else bitter antagonists for near a century. Marx and Freud have affected our culture to an extent that is still immeasurable. Nietzsche, a very sick man writing in a remote mountain retreat, is generally regarded

by Germans as having initiated a new 'post-Nietzschean' philosophy (Heidegger). Wittgenstein and Heidegger exerted a fascination upon those who knew them. Jaspers in a quiet way drew
many threads together, and, although criticized for retiring to
Basel during the war, was singled out by the American occupation
forces to reform the German universities in their zone. The Frankfurt School has forcibly brought home to us the limitations of
positivism or scientism.

The most outstanding feature of the whole German tradition, as
I suggested in the Introduction, is that it has been anthropocentric
in a broad sense, has always taken it to be the job of philosophy to
consider the whole embodied person in his environment of nature,
history and society. In spite of the great contributions of Leibniz,
Frege and Wittgenstein, it has not been much concerned with
technical logic; nor, except for Herbart, Freud and the Gestaltists, with questions of psychological detail. It has viewed man
as essentially active, and viewed the fact that he is capable of
moral action as especially significant. All modern books on ethics
are much concerned with what Kant had to say. Similarly,
modern books on the logic of science and the applicability of
mathematics, on observation and convention in science, can hardly
avoid referring to what Kant had to say. The person as an active
member of society, creator of works of art, subject of self-education
(culture=*Bildung*), was a concern that followed inevitably from
Kant's concern about morality. From Hegel onwards, German
philosophy was exercised to find a reconciliation between the
apparent deliverances of the natural sciences and the apparent
requirements of morality; and so was led into a far-reaching
discussion of the nature of religion and especially of the so-called
revealed religions of Judaism and Christianity. This resulted in
the assimilation of religion to philosophy in Hegel, and to the
vehement denunciations of Christianity by Mach, Nietzsche and
Freud.

This again, together with reflection upon moral man and his
society, led to the development of the new philosophy of history
and the new conception of history in the great German historians,
especially Burckhardt and von Ranke. From Herder, Hegel,

Dilthey and Weber derive in large measure the concepts needed for the sciences of sociology and linguistics.

Finally, the phenomenologists and existentialists have been concerned to find new ways of speaking of this development as a whole, to find a philosophy which can give a coherent account of man as receptive and as active, as product of nature yet also member of society, as product of history and yet individually creative. For the splitting off of the many new sciences, if such they should be called, such as sociology, linguistics, archaeology and scientific history, involves us in a re-thinking of the task of philosophy. This, I think, was above all the motivation of Husserl, Jaspers and the Frankfurt School.

I do not think it appropriate here to try to assess the influence of these philosophers upon the subsequent course of German and European history. The effect of such writings is but one factor among many that have to be evaluated by the serious historian, and the history of this century is still bedevilled by many myths, 'Western' and 'Eastern'. Those who know how the history of the First World War has fared will be cautious in their assertions about the causes of the Second World War.

What Then is Philosophy?

I hope this review of European philosophy since Descartes may have given some clue to an answer to this elusive question. It is a search for a satisfactory description of the relations between the most important factors in life. British analysis, French positivism, German activism all represent important trends or methods in this search. Yet the fact that one or another is emphasized in the master-pupil relation by which philosophy is mainly transmitted justifies us in speaking of 'traditions'.

One central task of all philosophy has always been to estimate the powers of human reasoning, and the extent of rationality – or something akin to it – in the world we live in. This has certainly been a central subject in all German philosophy. I would contend that it has established two propositions about the world and man. The first is that, try as we may to get at the ultimate facts, we find intervening an irremovable factor of human convention which is in part due to universal human modes of thought, in part to particular social and historical situations. There is such a conventional element in the most sophisticated science. But there is also a human or conventional element in our everyday view of the world, as the Gestaltists showed. Whether these 'humanized' facts are all that there is (positivism) or whether it makes sense to say that some of them point beyond themselves to that which is unknowable to us (transcendental – Kant, Jaspers), or at least unknowable in our epoch (transtemporal – Heidegger) – upon this there is no agreement. (I incline to agree with the latter view.)

The second proposition, connected with it, is that history is open-ended, that it makes no sense to ask either about the beginning of the world or its end or about its course as a whole. We can discern some rational patterns within the small slice of history known to us, but no more than that. This fact sets limits to the human imagination – we cannot, for example, really imagine what it would be like to be immortal. It calls for a review and critique of imaginative speculations (mythologies). Our human imaginations can never break entirely free from our experience. But the converse proposition is equally true; our human interpretations do tell us something true about nature and society. The limitations of language and culture are to be looked upon not as a shutter but as a veil or grid, which we can in great part understand and take account of in sizing up our experience.

Thus one of the chief tasks of philosophy is to provide a general orientation in the confusing world in which we live. Even in the times of Aristotle and Kant, but quite especially in our age, when 'science has got very complex',* it involves attempting to consider together the basic concepts and apparent trends of the sciences, along with those of other organized studies, such as archaeology and history, jurisprudence, textual criticism. None of the languages of the specialisms will do; philosophy must start from ordinary language, and to a certain extent invent its own. If philosophy opts

---

* *Plurimi pertransibunt et multiplex erit scientia*, the prophecy of *Daniel*, chapter 12, v. 5 (Vulgate), 'Many shall run to and fro and knowledge shall be increased' (A.V.) Inscription in Oxford University Library.

out of this task – as some English philosophers think it should – the result will merely be that some dogmatism, political, religious, or scientistic, will fill the vacuum.

But the chief task of this nature is to find ways of speaking about orientation-in-the-world and practical action together (with some splendid exceptions, English philosophy textbooks are either about theory of knowledge *or* about ethics). This task, always difficult, is particularly so in our sociological age, when we are constantly called upon to switch our attitude backwards and forwards from that of impartial observers of the social facts to that of committed agents acting into society. It is all too easy to put the blame for all one's shortcomings upon society, and take all the credit for one's achievements to oneself.

In this connection philosophy needs to continue the work begun by Schelling, Ernst Cassirer and Jaspers on the nature of mythological language and its relation to philosophy. We have to live with powerful social mythologies – the various forms of Christianity, communism, nationalism – as well as some fancy ones like scientology. Myth is a legitimate form of communication, especially with regard to what Jaspers called the great cyphers of love, conflict, death and suffering. It should be effective in changing personal attitudes; but it should not be confused with philosophy, in the stricter sense, which must aim to speak what is literally true, so far as that can be spoken. In our time myths have been effective in the founding of young people's communities. Mythologies must be judged by their results, be judged by standards that are in some extended sense rational, in that they have some relevance to our experience as a whole, and are not belied by the actions of those who profess them. What seems rather lacking at present is any vision capable of drawing together both halves of the civilized world, capable of re-forming live communities, local, regional and national, capable of inspiring the young both to individual enterprize and to constructive social experiment. It may be, as one German writer has suggested,* that man needs a private utopia for his immediate circle of family and friends and a public utopia for his life as a citizen, and that harm arises when the

* Arnold Gillen in *Merkur*, 1969.

standards arising from the one are applied to the other. It may be that the communist societies are more conscious of a public utopia, while people in the liberal-capitalist states have more sense of being governed by a private utopia, a sense of the desirable life for their immediate circle. Both are needed for the good life. A public mythology must include some sense for the value of law – in this both halves of the civilized world seem deficient, though in different ways.

The Christian mythology is an inescapable part of our Western cultural tradition, which we ignore at our peril. But the Christian myths are loosely connected, and it is possible, say, to adapt the Christmas, Easter, Eucharistic myths, while rejecting others. I personally suspect that all salvationist mythologies, claiming that one thing only is needful, such as belief in the saving sacrifice of Christ, in socialization of all means of production, in perfect sexual satisfaction, are harmful to an authentic life. Equally harmful are what have been called 'anti-utopias' – belief that someone antagonist, say Catholic or Fascist, is evil, to be destroyed absolutely. We have had plenty of reminders in our own day, through Stalin's and Hitler's camps, of how low human nature can sink. Nevertheless the division of men into the good and the evil, to the obliteration of all sense of common humanity, a feature of both Christian and communist mythology, results in the worsening of every conflict, as Nietzsche and Freud saw. We cannot expect, and should not wish, that society should function with the smoothness of clockwork – the ideal of the functionalist school of thought.

Harmful too is the myth that technology is all-powerful, and can finally conquer the wild element – the 'Shiva' element – in nature, that manifests itself in storms, hurricanes, earthquakes. Of course it can and should mitigate these; but every now and then nature shows its contempt for puny man, shows manifestly, as Kant insisted, that it is not arranged for human happiness. If we do candidly recognize this, we can find a certain grandeur in these natural phenomena – the theme of the *Book of Job*. I do not think this needs make us insensitive to the human fates involved – although there is certainly a tradition that has entered into common speech that taking things philosophically means maintaining a certain equilibrium in face of the joys and sorrows of life.

I have discussed these questions about myth and ideology because they have been to the fore lately. But I think the whole story of German philosophy is one of a gradual realization that the method of philosophy cannot be deductive, nor yet claim special self-evidence for its leading propositions. Plato's view of the soul as that which essentially sees the necessity of mathematical and quasi-mathematical propositions dominated European philosophy until Leibniz, and instilled the belief that a work of philosophy ought to consist of a string of deductively-connected propositions. So each of these writers' views of the world, of its law-abidingness and its chanciness, its joys and its miseries, tended to be pressed into this form – but was always breaking out of it. They all end up with the conviction that science is not reducible to logic, nor morality deducible from fact, and that knowledge and action are inextricably mixed up. From Hegel onwards, they recognize that neither knowledge nor action is intelligible except as social, as involving language, conventions, institutions, persons with bodies that are expressive and communicating with one another. That is not to deny that in and through these we can discover and communicate on the basis of a common humanity. Kant was the first to maintain that the world as we know it is 'humanized', and points beyond itself to much that we do not know.

It is a development which, so far as one can tell, is not finished. Our culture still seems able to bring forth works that are sufficiently within the tradition to be called philosophy. There is still a place for criticism of overweening specialist pretensions; for analysis of the change constantly taking place in the meanings of current categories and fundamental concepts; for imaginative portrayal of the philosopher's experience of man and his place in nature (Broad). In our time especially the exploration of instincts or drives by animal ethology and depth-psychology, and of the varieties of practical reasoning by statistical sociology, theory of games and futurology, call for attempts at a philosophical orientation.

The place of the individual in face of the social institutions which he helps to make, yet which largely make him, is far from clear, and beliefs about this have the gravest practical consequences. It seems unlikely that individual human decision will be swallowed up by physical or historical determinism; rather that it will continue to seem important and will be seen to be capable, within certain limits which we do not yet understand (but to which the concepts of cybernetics and information theory furnish some clues), of dominating its body and its immediate environment.*

If philosophy is neither a catalogue of forms of deductive reasoning, nor a deduction from self-evident truths, what is it? If, as seems to be the case, it is a kind of literature, concerned with the same sort of issues as much drama and poetry, what can we say is its distinctive form? I suggest it is akin to that of the guidebook; it aims to lay bare the system of concepts with which a certain age or culture interprets its experience; possibly to discover some very fundamental modes of interpretation ('structuralism'), possibly to suggest alternative ways of thinking which would make some tracts of life more intelligible than they are now. To use terms introduced by Professor Strawson, it should comprise both 'descriptive' and 'revisionary' metaphysics, tentative though these must be. It is bound to start from the familiar concepts of a certain epoch or culture; it is most unlikely that these will be suited to interpret a radically different culture: for example, it has proved so far impossible, even for the Indian Minister of Education,[3] to produce a really unified philosophy covering the European and the Indian ways of thinking and observing, although of course Indians utilize both. Philosophy, however, through its historical study of

---

* Cybernetics furnishes a clue by introducing the novel concept of a special kind of causal law, which one could call 'an equilibrating causal law'. It comes into operation in certain circumstances, holds only within certain limits, but within these is the primary determinant of a whole train of events. Much of both the physiological and the psychological aspects of personality are illuminated in terms of this conception. Information-theory introduces the novel concept of explaining what occurs by reference to what can be anticipated as probable. Also, information must be carried by some sufficient form of physical energy, but the laws governing it are fundamentally independent of the physical energy required. This concept also illuminates physiological and psychological features of personality. I emphasize that they merely furnish some clues.

the tradition, should be of interest to men of other ages and cultures, as a good guidebook often is. But it cannot achieve a 'God's-eye-view', valid for all time. Again, as a good guide book may reflect the writer's predominant interest in food or in architecture, so a good philosophy book may reflect the writer's predominant interest in perception or ethics, provided the whole of which these are but part – the person and his environment – is kept in view, as a good guidebook aims to reflect the spirit of a country or city as a whole.

This is the truth of what Plato meant by calling the philosopher 'spectator of all time and of all existence'. Literally taken, this is both impossible and one-sided; if he does no more than speak and write, the philosopher must act *into his own time*. Nor can we ever hope to deduce with certainty (as Plato thought) how we ought to act. Certainly life sometimes looks like 'little dogs biting one another, and little children quarrelling, laughing and then straightway weeping again' (Marcus Aurelius). But trying to look at many sides of life as Plato, Marcus Aurelius, Spinoza, Kant and Nietzsche did may breed – so Kant said – not happiness but a certain contentment.[4] And if we search for the truth, in facts and in traditions, with the passion they felt about it, we shall – though this may be a philosopher's prejudice – be the more likely to hit upon what we ought to do.

References

Introduction: Are there National Traditions in Philosophy?

1 Hobbes, *Leviathan*, ch. 5.
2 Hobbes, *Leviathan*, ch. 11.
3 Spinoza, *Works* or *Opera*, *Ethica*.
4 Spinoza, *Works* or *Opera*, bks IV and V, *passim*.
5 Hume, *Inquiry Concerning Human Understanding*, p. 165.
6 Gellner, *Thought and Change*, p. 74; cf. p. 143.

1. The Philosophy of the German Enlightenment: Leibniz and Kant

1 Marcel, *The Philosophy of Existence*, pp. 8 ff.
2 Kant, *Gesammelte Schriften*, vol. III.
3 Kant, *Critique of Practical Reason*, bk I, ch. 1, p. 30.
4 Kant, *Critique of Pure Reason*, p. 472.
5 Kant, *Critique of Judgement*, sec. 83.
6 Kant, *Critique of Judgement*, p. 406. *The Moral Law*, *Grundlegung*, p. 80.
7 Kant, *The Moral Law*, pp. 83f.
8 Kant, *The Moral Law*, ch. 3, p. 94.
9 Cf. Kant, *Critique of Pure Reason*, p. 381.
10 Cf. Kant, *Critique of Judgement*, pp. 382f. app. sec. 87.
11 Kant, *Prolegomena to any Future Metaphysic*, p. 118.
12 Kant, *Prolegomena*, p. 115.

13 Kant, *Gesammelte Schriften*, vol. VIII, p. 250.
14 Kant, *Gesammelte Schriften*, vol. VIII.

2. The German Enlightenment : Lessing, Herder and Weimar

1 Herder, *Werke* or *Reflections on the History of Mankind*.
2 Langer, *Philosophy in a New Key*, ch. 4.
3 Schiller, *Schillers Philosophische Schriften*, cf. Findlay, *Hegel, A Re-examination*, p. 690.
4 Goethe, *Poetry and Truth*, pt IV, bk 20.

3. From Enlightenment to Romanticism : German Idealism

1 Hume, *Treatise of Human Nature*, p. 415.
2 Hume, *Treatise of Human Nature*, p. 418.

4. German Idealism : Fichte, Schelling and Hegel

1 Copleston, *History of Philosophy*, vol. VII, p. 33; cf. chs 1–13.
2 Kaufmann, *Hegel*, p. 168.
3 Hegel, *Philosophy of History*, quoted Kaufmann, *Hegel*, p. 70.
4 Findlay, *Hegel, A Re-examination*, p. 151.
5 Hegel, *Philosophy of History*, Introduction.

5. The Aftermath of German Idealism: (1) Schopenhauer and Nietzsche

1 Schopenhauer, *Sämmtliche Werke, Die Welt als Wille und Vorstellung*; or *The World as Will and Idea*.
2 Nietzsche, *The Portable Nietzsche*, p. 146.
3 Nietzsche, *The Portable Nietzsche*, p. 225.
4 e.g. Macbeath, *Experiments in Living*.
5 e.g. Gellner, *Thought and Change*.
6 Nietzsche, *Werke, zur Genealogie der Moral*, Dritte Abhandlung, sec. 15.

7   Nietzsche, *Werke, Also sprach Zarathustra*, pt III, sec.
    'Von alten und neuen Tafeln', § 11; or *The Portable
    Nietzsche*, p. 315.

6. *The Aftermath of German Idealism: (2) Feuerbach and Marx*

1   Nietzsche, *Werke, Also sprach Zarathustra*, pt II, 'Die
    Stillste Stunde'; or *The Portable Nietzsche*, p. 258.
2   von Stein, *Begriff und Wesen der Gesellschaft*.

7. *Freud*

1   E. von Hartmann, *The Philosophy of the Unconscious*.
2   Cf. Brown, *Freud and the Post-Freudians*.
3   Freud, *New Introductory Lectures*, ch. 31.
4   Conze, *Buddhist Scriptures*, p. 187.
5   Freud, *New Introductory Lectures*, ch. 35.

8. *Linguistic Philosophy: Frege, the Vienna Circle, Wittgenstein
    and Dilthey*

1   Popper, *Logik der Forschung*, p. 111.
2   Wittgenstein, *Philosophische Untersuchungen*, pp. 88, 226.
3   Wittgenstein, *Philosophische Untersuchungen*, p. 45; also p. 49.
4   Wittgenstein, *Philosophische Untersuchungen*, p. 50.
5   Wittgenstein, *Philosophische Untersuchungen*, p. 50.
6   Whatmough, *Language*, p. 213.

9. *From Essentialism to Existentialism: Husserl, the Gestaltists
    and Heidegger*

1   Heidegger, *Being and Time*, p. 27.
2   Heidegger, *Being and Time*, p. 146.
3   Heidegger, *Being and Time*, p. 111.

10. Jaspers

1 Schilp, *Philosophy of Karl Jaspers*, p. 38.
2 Toulmin, *Uses of Argument*, p. 13.
3 Jaspers, *Philosophie* and *Von der Wahrheit*, pp. 208, 225.
4 Jaspers, *Von der Wahrheit*, p. 468.

11. One-Dimensional Man and the Principle of Hope

1 Phillpotts, *Edda and Saga.*
2 Horkheimer, *Eclipse of Reason*, German ed.
3 Habermas, *Theorie und Praxis* and *Erkenntnis und Interesse.*
4 MacIntyre, *Marcuse.*
5 Dahrendorf, *Essays in the Theory of Society*, ch. 4.
6 Auden, *Secondary Worlds.*

12. The Contribution of the German Tradition in Philosophy

1 Murdoch, *Sartre, Romantic Rationalist.*
2 MacIntyre, *Against the Self-Images of the Age*, and Winch, *The Idea of a Social Science.*
3 S. Radhakrishnan, *History of Philosophy, Eastern and Western.*
4 Cf. Kant, *Critique of Practical Reason*, p. 119.

Bibliography

Original philosophical texts and available English translations or paraphrases.

Adorno, T., *Negative Dialektik* (1956).

Ayer, A., *Language, Truth and Logic* (London 1936, latest edn 1967).

Bloch, Ernst, *Geist der Utopie* (Frankfurt 1963).

Bloch, Ernst, *Prinzip der Hoffnung* (Leipzig and Munich 1954–9).

Böhme, J., *A Study*, ed. Stroudt (Philadelphia 1957) (Selections).

Dahrendorf, R., *Class and Class-Conflict in Industrial Society* (London 1965).

Dahrendorf, R., *Essays in the Theory of Society* (London 1968).

Dilthey, W., *Gesammelte Schriften* (Leipzig 1923–58).

Dilthey, W., *Meaning in History*, tr. and ed. Rickman (London 1961).

Feuerbach, L., *The Essence of Christianity*, tr. Eliot (New York 1957).

Fichte, J. G., *The Science of Knowledge*, tr. Kroeger (London 1889).

Fichte, J. G., *The Science of Rights*, tr. Kroeger (London 1889).

Fichte, J. G., *Addresses to the German Nation*, tr. Jones and Turnbull (Chicago 1922).

Fichte, J. G., *Werke*, ed. Fromann (Stuttgart–Cannstadt 1964: incomplete).

Frege, G., *Translations from the Philosophical Writings of G. Frege*, ed. Geach and Black (Oxford 1960).

Freud, S., *Psychopathology of Everyday Life* (Vienna 1901; London 1960).

Freud, S., *Five Lectures on Psychoanalysis* (Vienna 1910).

Freud, S., *Introductory Lectures on Psychoanalysis* (Vienna 1917).

Freud, S., *Beyond the Pleasure-Principle* (London 1919).

Freud, S., *New Introductory Lectures on Psychoanalysis* (London 1933).

Freud, S., *Gesammelte Werke* (London 1940–60).

Freud, S., *Complete Psychological Works* (London 1953–   ).

Gadamer, H. G., *Wahrheit und Methode* (Tübingen 1965).

Goethe, J. W. von, *Dichtung und Wahrheit* (Leipzig 1922), tr. as *Poetry and Truth*, Smith (London 1913), or Oxenford (London 1904).

Goethe, J. W. von, *Werke* (Berlin 1953–   ).

Habermas, J., *Theorie und Praxis* (Neuwied and Berlin 1967).

Habermas, J., *Erkenntnis und Interesse* (Frankfurt 1968).

Habermas, J., *Technik und Wissenschaft als Ideologie* (Frankfurt 1968).

Hartmann, Eduard von, *The Philosophy of the Unconscious*, tr. Coupland (London 1931).

Havemann, R., *Dialektik ohne Dogma* (Reinbek bei Hamburg 1964).

Hegel, G. W. F., *Philosophy of History*, tr. Sibree (London 1861).

Hegel, G. W. F., *Lectures on the History of Philosophy*, trs. Haldane and Simpson (London 1892–6).

Hegel, G. W. F., *Philosophy of Fine Art*, tr. Osmaston (London 1920).

Hegel, G. W. F., *Science of Logic*, tr. Johnston and Struthers (London 1929).

Hegel, G. W. F., *Phenomenology of Mind*, tr. Baillie (London 1931).

Hegel, G. W. F., *Philosophy of Right*, tr. Knox (Oxford 1942).

Hegel, G. W. F., *Early Theological Writings*, tr. Knox (Chicago 1948).

Hegel, G. W. F., *Sämmtliche Werke*, eds Lassion and Hoffmeister (Hamburg 1952–   ).

Hegel, G. W. F., *Encyclopaedia of Philosophy*, tr. Mueller (New York 1959).

Hegel, G. W. F., *Philosophy of Mind*, tr. Miller (Oxford 1971).

Heidegger, M., *Sein und Zeit* (Halle 1931), tr. as *Being and Time*, Macquarrie and Robinson (Oxford 1967).

Heidegger, M., *Vom Wesen des Grundes* (Halle 1929).

Heidegger, M., *Was ist Metaphysik?* (Frankfurt 1949).

Heidegger, M., *What is Philosophy?* tr. Kluback and Wild (London 1958).

Herder, J. G. von, *Werke*, ed. Matthias (Leipzig 1903).

Herder, J. G. von, *Reflections on the History of Mankind*, tr. Manuel (Chicago 1968).
Also in Clark, R. T., *Herder, his Life and Thought* (California 1955) (Selections).

Hobbes, T., *Leviathan*, ed. Molesworth, 1839; many modern editions or paraphrases.

Horkheimer, Max, *Eclipse of Reason* (New York 1947); included with other material in *Kritik der instrumentellen Vernunft* (Frankfurt 1967).

Horkheimer, Max and Adorno, T., *Dialektik der Aufklärung* (1947).

Hume, D., *Treatise of Human Nature*, ed. Selby-Bigg (London 1896).

Hume, D., *Inquiry Concerning Human Understanding*, ed. Selby-Bigg (London 1894).

Husserl, E., *Ideen zu einer reinen Phänomenologie* (Halle 1922).

Husserl, E., *Ideas*, tr. Gibson (London 1931).

Husserl, E., *Cartesian Meditations*, tr. Cairns (The Hague 1960).

Husserl, E., *Crisis of European Sciences*, tr. Carr (Evanston 1940).

Jaspers, K., *Philosophie* (Berlin 1932). *Philosophy*, tr. Ashton (Chicago 1971).

Jaspers, K., *Von der Wahrheit* (Munich 1952).

THE GERMAN TRADITION IN PHILOSOPHY

Jaspers, K., *Vom Ursprung und Ziel der Geschichte* (Zurich 1949), tr. as *The Origin and Goal of History*, Bullock (London 1953).

Jaspers, K., *Man in the Modern Age*, tr. E. and C. Paul (London 1933, 1951).

Jaspers, K., *The Perennial Scope of Philosophy*, tr. Mannheim (London 1950).

Jaspers, K., *Way to Wisdom*, tr. Mannheim (London 1951).

Jaspers, K., *Tragedy is Not Enough*, tr. Reiche and others (London 1953).

Jaspers, K., *Reason and Existence*, tr. Earle (London 1956).

Jaspers, K., *The Future of Germany*, tr. Ashton (Chicago, 1957).

Jaspers, K., *Die grossen Philosophen* (Munich 1957), tr. as *The Great Philosophers* (London and New York 1962–6).

Jaspers, K., *Der Philosophische Glaube angesichts der Offenbarung* (Munich 1962), tr. as *Philosophical Faith and Revelation* (Chicago 1971).

Kant, I., *Gesammelte Schriften* (Berlin 1910–).

Kant, I., *Critique of Judgement*, tr. Bernard (London 1914).

Kant, I., *Critique of Pure Reason*, tr. N. Kemp Smith (London 1933).

Kant, I., *Religion Within the Bounds of Reason Alone*, trs. Greene and Hudson (New York 1934).

Kant, I., *Prolegomena to any Future Metaphysic*, tr. P. G. Lucas (Manchester 1953).

Kant, I., *Critique of Practical Reason*, tr. L. W. Beck (New York 1956).

Kant, I., *The Moral Law* (*Grundlegung*), tr. H. J. Paton (Oxford 1961).

Koffka, F., *Principles of Gestalt Psychology* (London 1935, 1962).

Köhler, W., *Gestalt Psychology* (London 1930).

Leibniz, G. W., *Sämmtliche Werke*, ed. Rechl (Darmstadt 1924).

Leibniz, G. W., *Philosophy of Leibniz* (London 1934) (Selection).

Leibniz, G. W., *Selections*, ed. and tr. P. P. Wiener (New York 1951).

196

Lessing, G. E., *Theological Writings*, tr. H. Chadwick (London 1956).

Lessing, G. E., *Sämmtliche Schriften* (Berlin 1968).

Mach, E., *Erkenntnis und Irrtum* (Leipzig 1926).

Malcolm: *A Memoir*, with G. H. von Wright, *Wittgenstein, A Biographical Sketch* (London 1958).

Mannheim, K., *Ideology and Utopia* (London 1936; latest edn

Marcuse, H., *Eros and Civilisation* (Munich 1955, 1967).

Marcuse, H., *One-Dimensional Man* (London 1964).

Marcuse, H., *Psychology, Politics and Utopia* (London 1970).

Marx-Engels, *Gesamtausgabe* (Moscow 1927) includes MSS of 1844 in vol. 1. 3).

Marx, Karl, *Selected Writings in Sociology and Social Philosophy*, ed. and tr. Bottomore and Rubel (London 1956).

Marx, Karl, *Die Früschriften*, ed. Landshut (Stuttgart 1920).

Nietzsche, F., *Ausgewählte Werke*, ed. Messer (Cologne 1930).

Nietzsche, F., *Werke*, ed. Schechta (Munich 1954–65).

Nietzsche, F., *The Portable Nietzsche*, tr. W. Kaufmann (New York 1954).

Nietzsche, F., *Zarathustra*, tr. Tille and Bozman (London 1958).

Novalis, *Schriften* (Leipzig 1929).

Popper, K., *Logik der Forschung* (Vienna 1935); tr. as *The Logic of Scientific Discovery* (London 1959).

Sartre, J.-P., *L'Imaginaire* (Paris 1948).

Schelling, F. W. J., *Werke* (Munich 1927–59) (nothing of importance translated).

Schelling, F. W. J., *Grösse und Verhängnis* (Munich 1955).

Schiller, J. C. F., *Schillers Philosophische Schriften* (Leipzig 1951).

Jaspers, *Philosophy of Karl Jaspers*, ed. Schilp (New York 1957).

Schopenhauer, A., *Sämmtliche Werke* (Munich, 1911–42).

Schopenhauer, A., *The World as Will and Idea*, tr. E. F. Payne (Indian Hills 1958).

Spinoza, B., *Works*, tr. Elwes (London 1884).

Spinoza, B., *Opera*, ed. Gebhardt (Heidelberg 1926).

Weber, Max, *Wirtschaft u. Gesellschaft* (Tübingen 1947),

Weber, Max, *Gesammelte Aufsätze zur Wissenschaftslehre* (Tübingen 1968).

Wittgenstein, L., *Tractatus-Logico-Philosophicus* (interleaved translation, London 1922); German with interleaved translation by Pears and McGuiness (London 1961).

Wittgenstein, L., *Philosophische Untersuchungen*, German with interleaved translation by Anscombe (Oxford 1958).

Index

INDEX